AN
ILLUSTRATED
HISTORY
OF FRENCH
CUISINE

Photo Camponogara

A Citizen of Lyon at table 17 centuries ago

AN ILLUSTRATED HISTORY OF FRENCH CUISINE

From Charlemagne to Charles de Gaulle

by
CHRISTIAN GUY

Translated by
Elisabeth Abbott

BRAMHALL HOUSE   NEW YORK

LIBRARY OF CONGRESS CATALOG Card Number 62-15020

Copyright © 1962 by Les Productions de Paris

This edition published by Bramhall House,
a division of Clarkson N. Potter, Inc., by
arrangement with The Orion Press, Inc.
(A)

Menu

First Course

Charlemagne, first *grand seigneur* of the table. The Best Morsel to the Bravest. The Use of Skulls as Drinking Cups Goes Out. The Merovingians Disliked Bland Food. The Trencher, or the Art of Eating Bread. At Last, Women Are Allowed to Sit at the Table. The Emperor Mistrusts the Potency of Wine. The Original Recipe for Flaming Peacock.

Second Course

A Chef Named Taillevent. How Can One Eat Little Children! The Apotheosis of Whale Meat. Joan of Arc Ate Five Soups at a Time. What You Should Know about M. Taillevent. Who Was the Author of the "Ménagier de Paris?" Agnès Sorel, First Royal Mistress to Entertain Royally. Thanks to Jacques Cœur We Eat Turkey.

Third Course

The Fabulous Era of Catherine de' Medici. François I Likes Veal, Henri II Prefers Snails. The Bishop of Sens Sets the Fashion for Donkey Meat. The King Drinks, but Fears Intoxication and Poison. What Montaigne Thought of Cooks. A Poet Gives Us a Salad.

Fourth Course

Henri IV Did Not Invent "Chicken-in-the-pot." Thank You, Monsieur Serres. Serres Encouraged the Peasants to Stay Home. Two Recipes for Good King Henri's "Chicken-in-the-pot." Lavarenne, Cook and Confidential Agent. The Technique of Boiling an Egg.

Fifth Course

Louis XIV, the Most Illustrious Glutton. Thanks to Coffee, Business Flourishes in Marseille. Dom Pérignon, Ancestor of Père Gaucher. The Vatel Enigma. Bread Becomes Important.

Sixth Course

The "Petits Soupers": Wit Bubbles in Casseroles and Champagne in Glasses. Meals Are Served with Clock-like Precision. Courtiers, Both Men and Women, Take to the Kitchen.

Seventh Course

Parmentier Gives France Its National Vegetable. Parmentier: a Prisoner Who Does not Come Back Empty-handed. Louis XVI Thinks Only of Eating. The French Cuisine is Enriched by Beefsteak.

Eighth Course

Napoléon is Better on Horseback than at the Table. All Parisians at the Same Table. Soupless Suppers Except in Méas. The "Napoléon of Preserved Food" is also Betrayed by the English. All the Secrets of "Chicken *à la Marengo*." Laguipière, Head Cook in the Imperial Kitchens. A Perfect Gentleman: the Marquis Louis de Cussy.

Ninth Course

Cambacérès and Grimod de la Reynière. No Guest is Late at the Arch-Chancellor's Dinners. How the Arch-Chancellor Issued His Invitations. The Illustrious Carême and His Slanders. The Most Fantastic Host of All. How to Judge One's Real Friends. There Is Nothing (At a Dinner) Like Those Ladies of the Théâtre Français. He Died in the Château de la Brinvilliers. Some of de la Reynière's Epicurean Rules.

Tenth Course

Talleyrand and Brillat-Savarin. All the Clergy of Autun are Guilty of Gourmandise. Talleyrand "Hunter of Beavers." Talleyrand and the Salmon. Brillat-Savarin, an Uninteresting Guest. Louis XVI is the Murderer of Brillat-Savarin. The Aphorisms of Brillat-Savarin.

Eleventh Course

Sugar is Introduced. Benjamin Delessert, the First Sugar King. Prince Kurakine, Ambassador and Gastronome. The Best Were His Masters. He is Always in Good Kitchens.

Twelfth Course

A Gourmet King and Two Monarchs without Appetite. "Jewels" and Scraps. The Murderer à la Fourchette. From the Lover of Soups to the Man with the Saucers. A King of the Table: Louis XVIII. A War Correspondent Sets the Fashion for Couscous in Paris. Louis-Philippe Eats Like a Cheap-Jack. In Future Ask for a "Montmireil à la Béarnaise."

Thirteenth Course

When the Father of the Three Musketeers Dines. Everything is Ready When Mademoiselle Mars Arrives. Mademoiselle George Peels the Truffles Herself. Salad à la Alexandre Dumas, Père. Duval Supplied the Meat. The End of Romantic Kitchens. Admirable Sophie, Dr. Véron's Cook. The Host Owed his Fortune to a Chest Salve.

Fourteenth Course

Baron Brisse Is Not a Horseman. Baron Brisse and his Three Hundred and Sixty-six Menus. Brisse Misses his Last Dinner. At Nohant, the Most Attractive Dining Room in the World. Sainte-Beuve: the Good Friday Scandal.

Fifteenth Course

Charles Monselet, the Gastronome with the Club-foot. He Forgets Émilie for the Pleasures of the Table.

Sixteenth Course

A Frenchman Invents Margarine. A Method for Transforming Margarine into Butter. The Academy of Sciences against Margarine. Rat Meat...? Why, It's Very Good. Cat is a Fine Tidbit, but Dog is Tough. He Dedicates his Cooking to the Virgin and Invents Lobster à l'Américaine.

Seventeenth Course

A Bavarian Clergyman Would Have the French Eat More Wisely. A King of the Earth: Jules Gouffé. Paput-Lebeau's Advice. Sebastian Kneipp's Good Food. Félix Faure Devours a Leg of Capon. Controversy Over a Menu at the Élysée.

Eighteenth Course

The Mayors' Banquet Does not Stop People from Talking about Cassoulet. A Cannon Shot Marks a Historic Date. Twenty Cassoulets... Only One Secret.

Nineteenth Course

Léon Daudet, Experienced Gastronome, Organizes the First Goncourt Luncheon. The Cruel Fate of a Futurist Cook.

Twentieth Course

After the 1918 Armistice French Cuisine Turns Democratic. For Brillat-Savarin, a Pious Thought and a Banquet. He Cooks Mutton the Way Carême Did. The Famous "Evenings" of the "Crapouillot."

Twenty-first Course

Curnonsky, Grand Seigneur and Prince. The Chaud-froid Killed its Grandfather. He had no Dining Room in which to Receive his Friends. His Best Venture: the Academy of Gastronomes. A Fortune at Riec-sur-Belon. He Classified Gastronomes.

RECIPIENT FOR " CERVOISE " (BEER OF ANCIENT GAUL), GALLO-ROMAN PERIOD
(Photo Josse Lalance)

First Course

CHARLEMAGNE, FIRST GRAND SEIGNEUR OF THE TABLE

One afternoon in the month of September, 774 A.D., a little band of men-at-arms were riding through the Ile-de-France: Charlemagne and his valiant knights returning home from Italy. Because of a woman the king of the Franks had been forced to hasten south and give battle. Now he was coming back without the faithless one, but with an additional crown to his glory—the crown of the Lombards.

The sun was setting. The horses showed signs of exhaustion, and their riders, having miscalculated the length of the route, were now obliged to give up hope of reaching Paris before the following day.

As they came to a crossroads, Charlemagne raised his arm: his companions gathered around him, all eyes turned towards the countenance of the future emperor whose mouth and shaved chin were framed in a thick, black, flowing mustache. At that moment a swineherd, leading his drove from oak-grove to oak-grove, came in sight. One of the riders hailed him.

" Tell us, friend, do you know of a monastery or a parish whose prior would be well enough provided with food to receive us? "

The man studied his questioner, then

answered slowly: " You'll find food and lodging not far from here. There's a monastery with kind and friendly monks. They aren't rich, but the prior will be able to refresh you. "

The band of warriors resumed their march. In a little while they came to the gate of a monastery which might well be, as some of them claimed, the monastery of Reuil-en-Brie. The prior received them in person, but when he recognized Charlemagne, his face reflected both joy and anxiety. Joy at having before him the bold warrior of Christianity; anxiety at having to " refresh, " as the swineherd had said, so important a personage whose reputation for being a heavy eater was already well established. As for the king's companions, thought the prior, one had only to look at them to know that they were not men to lag behind their emperor in the pleasures of the table.

Now the resources of that little community were limited. The abbot ordered up from the cellars some of those marvelous cheeses the fame of which in later years was to spread far beyond the borders of Brie. Charlemagne and his knights feasted well. At the first mouthfuls, however, every one of them made the mistake of removing the crust. One of the monks respectfully called their attention to this error; whereupon the gentlemen abstained and willingly agreed that the advice was excellent.

" I thought I knew everything that could be eaten, " exclaimed Charlemagne before the end of the meal. " It was only vanity on my part... I have just discovered in this cheese one of the most delectable foods imaginable. " And he added: " I desire that twice a year a goodly quantity of these cheeses of Brie be brought to my palace at Aix-la-Chapelle... And I pray you to see to it especially that they have a good consistency—and also a good crust! "

THE BEST MORSEL TO THE BRAVEST

The future emperor's astonishment was not feigned. If Charlemagne was not a gastronome or a gourmet in the sense those words have attained in later years, he was nevertheless a lord of the table to whom French cookery owes some of its earliest titles to pre-eminence.

Today only grammar school pupils observe the memory of Charlemagne. That is a lacuna. Others should sing his praises too, those whose eyes shine at the sight of an exquisitely laid table or whose faces beam and light up at the mere mention of a delectable dish.

Before Charlemagne's day, people ate a great deal, but they ate poorly.

An abundance of food compensated for lack of variety on the tables of the Gauls. Meats were usually cooked on spits: chiefly fresh pork or poultry (goose for the most part), which people raised themselves. Near the sea or near rivers, meat was replaced by fish which was grilled when it was of a good size, but more often simply boiled.

Meals were long: the Gauls loved to feast and carouse. Their tables were set up near a brazier on which were spits and cauldrons filled with boiling water in which meat and fish were cooked together. Not till much later did it become the custom to cook them separately. Tables were very low—usually a broad stone set flat on the bare ground, around which the diners sat on bundles of wood, straw or hay. Later, at the time of the Roman invasion, the victors tried to accustom the Gauls to reclining while they ate. But they were not successful. However, the Gauls consented to discard their bundles of hay for low stools.

Food was served in a cleanly fashion on copper dishes in the houses of the rich, in earthenware or wooden bowls in the houses of the poor. The noblest courtesies of the table date from that period. It was the custom for the host to carve the main dish himself—reindeer, wild oxen or wild boar—and pointedly offer the best piece to the guest he wished to honor or whom he considered the bravest of all—a choice that did not always please the others. Jealousy fomented bitter quarrels, which often ended in fights to the death. The fighting, however, was never known to interrupt the meals.

The ordinary beverage was an infusion of barleywater; people sometimes drank wine, but beer was the favorite until the seventeenth century. It is not known whether the beer which the Celts consumed was a national brew or a foreign import. It was made with barley and, as were their wines and infusions, mixed with honey, and drunk from the horns of aurochs or wild bulls, or even from bowls hollowed out of human skulls.

THE USE OF SKULLS AS DRINKING CUPS GOES OUT

The conquest of Gaul by the Romans brought to the table of the Gauls more varied refinements than any real gastronomical changes. In later years Antonin Carême was to write that " the Roman Cuisine was fundamently barbaric. " That Lamartine-of-the-kitchen was not wrong. Though the Roman cuisine was lavish, it was totally without refinement.

Picture the guests reclining comfortably on couches, regaling themselves with sows stuffed with ingredients ranging from fish to field flowers. A host of those days served his guests a

17

ragoût of tongues of birds that " had all sung sweetly in their lifetime! " Or perhaps a ragoût of crows' brains accompanied by peas mixed with corn and lentils *aux pierres précieuses*!

The Romans taught the Gauls the use of spices—cumin, pepper, ginger—which added greatly to the savor of their meats. In return they benefited by a vast number of innovations and discoveries. No sooner had Gaul been conquered than the Celts were exporting to Rome geese, hams and various sausages and *foies gras* that were the delight of transalpine gastronomes. And oysters, which were sent to Rome in regular tank carts.

The Romans also taught their " colonials " better table manners. On their initiative the Gauls gave up drinking out of aurochs' horns and human skulls. The use of a single cup that was passed from guest to guest became custom. When the cup was empty, a woman brought in another, filled with the wine of Beziers or Vienne, with beer or hydromel. Every village, every great family, had its exclusive recipe for hydromel.

THE MEROVINGIANS DISLIKED BLAND FOOD

After the Romans, when the Barbarians and other Franks overran the land of Gaul, nothing was added to French cooking which was already coming into its own. The new invaders had more to learn from the Gallo-Romans than the latter from them. The Merovingian lords had only one real passion: their plate, which was often of great value and which they took with them wherever they went. Each man's ambition was to own the most important collection.

Pope Julius I designated December 25th as the day on which Christmas would be celebrated—a decision that would have no place in this history of French cooking if the custom of midnight suppers on Christmas Eve and New Year's Eve had not been promptly inaugurated. In the beginning those suppers were an excuse to gather families and intimate friends around a table. Later on, in the Middle Ages, certain foods were traditionally served at that time in preference to others.

THE TRENCHER, OR THE ART OF EATING BREAD

But to return to Charlemagne. He was the first of the " Lords of the Table. " And in appearance he was

CAROLINGIAN REPAST

admirably suited to the role: a strong, broad-shouldered man, of a good height though not excessively tall, possessing a firm, vigorous step, a sensual mouth, a fairly large nose and a loud, clear voice. He had always enjoyed excellent health, but one day towards the end of his life his physicians prescribed a much stricter regime than the one to which he had been accustomed. The emperor is said to have flown into a violent rage, refused to keep the prescribed diet and thrown his physicians out of the door. Then, to calm his nerves, he ordered his servants to roast at once " three plump geese and the rump of the wild boar " he had killed the day before!

Quantity was still preferred to quality. And though pyramids of meats followed one after the other on tables, certain refinements, which we might call gastronomical, were introduced. Before those pyramids were " piled one on top of the other " and served, each diner was careful to place a thick slice of bread on his plate: the trencher to soak up the fats from meats, poultry and game. The Emperor Charlemagne was excessively fond of game. He himself was an intrepid hunter, and the word game dates from his day as the term for all the various animals killed in the hunt.

AT LAST, WOMEN ARE ALLOWED TO SIT AT THE TABLE

People ate twice a day: they breakfasted on awaking and dined about the middle of the afternoon. Even when the men were at war it was customary for them to observe a truce at meal times.

Among the rich, floral decorations played a prominent role. The table was often covered with a carpet of roses and field flowers instead of a table cloth. It was customary to wash one's hands before sitting down at the table.

Charlemagne was the first to invite women to sit at the table with men— but only on condition that they did not offend by nauseating odors or noxious perfumes.

When the cultivation of vegetables and fruit trees spread throughout the Ile-de-France and the valley of the Rhône, Charlemagne promulgated an ordinance regulating their culture. He also insisted that there should always be a plentiful supply of pike, eel and carp at his disposal in the vast fishponds he had ordered built in the environs of Paris.

Dinner was the most lavish meal of the day. It started with a salad of mallows or hops, garden herbs and various vegetables to excite the

20

appetite. Then, as a second course, great quantities of grilled meat and game of all sorts. At Charlemagne's table compote of fruit was served for the first time as an accompaniment to meats. People no longer ate with their fingers, but with the point of their knife.

Bread, made of rye, was still fairly poor. While the bread served at the monarch's table or at the tables of his lords was made with a certain care, the same cannot be said for the bread served to the people or to serfs in the country or in the slum quarters of towns where no rules—either hygienic or culinary—were observed. Rye can be extremely dangerous if eaten when a certain poisonous growth appears on its spike. It causes convulsions, which are known as St Anthony's fire or ergotism.

THE EMPEROR MISTRUSTS THE POTENCY OF WINE

In Charlemagne's day, the individual cup was unknown. People drank out of the samo goblet, passsing it from hand to hand and having it replenished by servants or the young daughters of the household. As an aperitif, they drank " mulled wine, " a light red wine, grown locally, which poets praised as the masterpiece of human ingenuity. According to them, it combined " the vigor and the aromatic savor of wine, the flavor and sweetness of honey and the perfume of pure, rich aromatics from distant lands. " This mulled wine was popularly believed to have astonishing aphrodisiacal properties, as were certain hydromels. Charlemagne, however, bluntly declared he had no faith in its remarkable virtues. The king may be said to have been fairly expert in that matter. He had four wives and a multitude of mistresses and between them they presented him with fifty children.

Charlemagne's favorite drink was cider made by the Normans. In his *Capitulary*, the sovereign recommended it to sufferers from gout or gravel. He liked wine, but drank it sparingly, mistrusting its potency.

THE ORIGINAL RECIPE FOR FLAMING PEACOCK

Among feathered birds and game the peacock was king. How did he get to the court of Charlemagne? History has never enlightened us. All that is known is that the peacock first appeared on the sovereign's table in the year 800, the very day when the Pope placed the crown of " Emperor of the West " on Charlemagne's head. For more than five hundred years this bird of tasteless and leathery flesh was to be considered by gourmets to be finer than the swan, the bittern or the stork.

At banquets peacocks were served whole. Instead of plucking the bird, cooks cleverly skinned it so that the feathers came off with the skin. The feet were then cut off, but were later attached to the thighs just before the dish was served. Next, the peacock was stuffed with aromatic spices and herbs. Before the bird was put on the spit, the head, with the feathers still on it, was wrapped in a piece of cloth or linen. During the cooking, the linen was kept damp to preserve the head in perfect condition. Finally, when the peacock was done, it was removed from the spit; the feet were re-attached, the cloth removed and the aigrette set in order. Skin and feathers were added, the tail spread out. At this point the mistress of the house filled the peacock's beak with cotton impregnated with camphor and set a light to it. " The bird arrives on the table spitting flames. "

TWO EXAMPLES OF GALLIC POTTERY
(Photo Giraudon)

SOME GALLIC AND FRANKISH RECIPES

LOIRS FARCIS   STUFFED DORMICE

Prepare the stuffing as follows: take the meat of a dormouse, cut it into small pieces and mix with ground pepper, cumin and ground nuts. Fill your dormice with this stuffing and after sewing them up, put them in the oven. They can also be stewed.

ESCARGOTS AU LAIT   SNAILS IN MILK

Take snails that have been fattened in milk. Sponge them and dry them carefully. Remove from the shells, and leave them for a day in salt water. Fry them in oil and do lightly with oleologarum; oleologarum is made with lovage, coriander, rue, broth, honey and a little oil. Or else with thyme, savory, pepper, honey, broth and oil.

VIN AUX ROSES (OU AUX VIOLETTES)   ROSE (OR VIOLET) WINE

Let roses (or violets) marinate seven days in wine. Take them out. Put fresh roses (or violets) in their place and leave to soak again for seven days. Strain the wine in which the flowers have steeped. And when ready to drink, add some honey to it.

SAUCE POUR LES LANGOUSTES ET LES CREVETTES
                    HOW TO COOK CRAYFISH AND SHRIMP

Wash and trim crayfish or shrimp and put them in an earthenware casserole. Add water, salt. Let this reduce by half and put it all in a cauldron with oil and broth, a bouquet of oregano and coriander. When this is almost done, add a little heated wine. Pour over it a mixture of honey, lovage, cumin, coriander, roots of benzoin, rue, caraway and vinegar. Bring to a boil. Place your crayfish (or shrimp) on a serving dish and pour the sauce over it.

SAUCE POUR LES MELONS   SAUCE FOR MELONS

Mix together pepper, mint, honey and wine, broth and vinegar. Benzoin (benjamin) is sometimes added.

SALTED-MEAT MERCHANT, XVth CENTURY *(Photo Josse Lalance)*

Second Course

A CHEF
NAMED TAILLEVENT

With the death of Charlemagne (813) the French cuisine slumbers. It will not come to life again until the advent of the first Valois at the beginning of the fourteenth century.

For five hundred years the art of good eating was confined to convents and monasteries: there it vegetated, in spite of the honorable efforts of certain priors and Mother Superiors. Prelates and monks gave up eating game in favor of pork meat which was always roasted on a spit. Braised meat and ragoûts were still unknown which is the same as saying that French cuisine was still like a bird that lacked a wing.

Since the death of Charlemagne famine had spread throughout the ancient territories of the Holy Empire. There had already been ominous signs of famine during the Emperor's long reign, but he had temporarily averted it by prohibiting the export of grain. This was a revolutionary decision at a time when certain other sovereigns were realizing enormous personal profits by shamelessly exporting grain harvested in their own countries. Charlemagne forbade the sale of grain *nimis care*—at too high a price—and set a maximum tariff for wheat as well as for barley and oats. And finally he ordered all his lords to take care that " their people did not die of hunger. "

" Let all the poor who, driven by hunger, have left their dwellings, be gathered together. No man has the right to maltreat them or to reduce them to serfdom: they enjoy the protection of the Emperor. "

Immediately after Charlemagne's death, the lords and the members of the clergy hastened to abolish those restraints which embarrassed them. For twenty years, they had been subject to a special tax known as " alms for the starving. " They now retaliated by establishing a frankly illicit trade—a " black market "—in the principal foodstuffs.

This then was the beginning of a famine that was to last for several centuries. It often co-existed with periods of great opulence, notably at the court of France, where it was felt that the presence of the monarch—ordained by the Lord—implied a " duty to display the greatest possible luxury. " But from those oases of opulence, the cuisine of France derived no benefit. No great chef, no artist of the palate, no cook of that era has left us so much as a trace of his culinary skill or his gastronomical knowledge.

HOW CAN ONE EAT LITTLE CHILDREN !

While men and women at the Court of France, in châteaux and in some cloisters, were guzzling without discernment and without taste, the country and even certain towns were ravaged by the cruelest want. To bake their bread, the peasants had to resort to mixing earth with the little flour they could find. Faced with that degrading situation, a few resourceful souls rebelled and set to work to discover more nourishing ingredients: instead of earth they used ox blood. This mixture they baked on a flat stone until it was hard, then they cut it into round cakes and pierced them with a hole in the middle in order to hang them up. Those cakes would keep for years.

Along with those attempts to make bread with ox blood, people tried to use acorns, leaves, even bark to replace cereals. But the French people of the Middle Ages, whose ancestors had been nourished solely on meat, did not take kindly to that vegetarian diet. They became wolves; they thought and acted like wolves. " Where is it written that only the flesh of oxen, pigs, goats and chickens is nourishing ?... That is merely an assumption! " exclaimed a scholar.

From that to cannibalism was but a step—a step which they took. There were men in France who made a habit of eating human flesh and this custom continued for three centuries. On this subject read what Raoul Glaber, that ribald monk of the eleventh century, who left half a dozen resounding reports, has to say:

26

" Cannibalism, " writes Glaber, " is rife particularly in certain sections of the center of France, the most underprivileged areas.

" On the highroads, the strong seize the weak; they tear them apart, roast them and eat them. Bands of men roam the countryside, generally in groups, attacking lonely wayfarers, but sparing peasants who are known in the region and whose disappearance would cause alarm.

" They even attack whole families of mountebanks and strolling minstrels, with their children, killing them and selling their flesh in the nearest market. "

Some of those monsters offered young children a piece of fruit and lured them aside to devour them. " This frightful frenzy, " Glaber remarks ironically, " went so far that animals were safer than men. "

At Tournos, he relates, a merchant displayed and sold human flesh for several months before he was arrested. At Macon an innkeeper cut the throats of unfortunate travelers who had begged asylum of him at night.

Those who have practiced cannibalism say that when you have once eaten human flesh, you acquire such a taste for it that you are tormented by the need to taste it again.

THE APOTHEOSIS OF WHALE MEAT

After five hundred years of lethargic slumber, the French cuisine opened one eye at the end of the thirteenth century. Even before the Valois, Philippe-le-Bel and Charles-le-Bel had done their best to abolish famine. To say that none of the three thought of putting an end to the illicit trade in grain, would not be true. If they themselves were not " involved, " they were nevertheless aware of clandestine transactions which their ministers merely winked at.

As the famine abated, however, the French gave more thought to improving their menus. Trade in food commodities was resumed on a grand scale. The Parisian housewife of the thirteenth century did not even have to leave her house to buy her daily provisions. Peddlers, leading an ass or carrying a basket, roamed the city. All day long the streets rang with their various familiar cries.

Shops were well stocked. Barges, loaded with food, lined the quays. For example... in Paris, which was a tedious journey from the coasts in those days, the fishmarkets were filled with salmon, turbot, brill, mullet, sole, dab, plaice, mackerel, whiting, haddock, sturgeon, weever, conger-eel, sardines, lobster, shrimps, mussels, codfish, red mullet...

This era was also the apotheosis of whale meat. In those days the great sea-mammals wandered close to the shores of France and throughout the Middle Ages vast quantities of them were eaten. Whale meat was the *crajois* or Lenten fare, one of the principal sources of food for the poor who were not discouraged at having to cook that tough meat at least twenty-four hours before it was edible.

Nowadays there is no more whale meat, at least in the French markets. The last time it was served was in 1892 in a Paris restaurant near the Halles Centrales. One of the guests, Dr. Félix Bremont, tells us:

" I can't say anything bad about that whale meat, but neither do I feel I can say much that is good. Take a piece of lean beef and boil it in water in which a stale mackerel has been washed, mix this broth with some sort of a piquant sauce and you'll have a dish similar to the one served me under the name of *Escalope de baleine à la Valois* (Escalope of whale à la Valois). "

JOAN OF ARC ATE FIVE SOUPS AT A TIME

The famous banquets of the Middle Ages do not appear until the Valois come to power in 1328. However, the Crusades had already introduced rice, buckwheat and a quantity of Oriental spices into France in addition to onion and garlic which the French had known since the Gallo-Roman period. Among the new spices were ginger, cinnamon, bay leaf, thyme, rosemary, scallions, shallots and anis. Pepper, which was introduced into France at the time of the Roman invasion, was the rarest of all: it still came from the distant Indies. There was a common expression, " as costly as pepper. " When a man won a lawsuit it was customary to thank the judge by presenting him with a fairly large package of that rare spice. This practice was so abused, however—the Paris magistrates were the " most costly in France "—that Charles VII flatly forbade it. For a long time after that, however, there were many backsliders—clandestine, of course.

Rice, buckwheat and various spices were not yet used to season soup which was then in its heyday. It was customary to serve three or four different soups at one meal. And it was not unusual for a dinner to consist of six, eight or even a dozen.

This passion for soup lasted until the reign of Louis XI, in fact down to the Renaissance. It was still in honor in Joan of Arc's day. Gilles de Retz, one of the Maid's closest companions, who preferred the raw entrails of infants whose stomachs he opened, tells us that " Jehanne put some wine in the bottom of a receptacle and poured four or five different soups over it. She never took anything else."

The basis of those soups was chiefly " cullis " (a thick meat juice or veal stock) like the *Potage à la Reine* that Taillevent prepared in the kitchens of Charles V. The following is the recipe:

Cook a chicken in white stock with a little rice. When it is done, bone the chicken and rub the meat through a fine sieve. Mix with the broth in which it was cooked and thicken with a little cream, some butter and the yolks of well-beaten eggs.

Those broths obviously made nourishing soups and one can easily understand why the Maid found them satisfying.

WHAT YOU SHOULD KNOW ABOUT M. TAILLEVENT

We have just mentioned the name of Taillevent, Guillaume Tirel, called Taillevent (1314?-1395), ancestor of the most celebrated French cooks. Taillevent is the author of the first *Viandier*, the oldest known cookbook. The second oldest is the *Ménagier de Paris*, written in the reign of Charles VI, towards 1392, at least five or ten years later.

In a manuscript dating from 1326 and relating to the coronation of Jeanne

COLLATION IN THE BATH *(Photo Josse Lalance)*

d'Evreux, Queen of France—the wife of Charles-le-Bel—the name of Taillevent appears for the first time. It is mentioned among the kitchen scullions. Lacking more definite information we would say that he must have been about twelve years old at that time.

After that we lose trace of him for twenty years. In 1346 he reappears in the service of Philippe VI of Valois, as head cook. Three years later, the sovereign presents him with a house at Saint-Germain-en-Laye (1), " in consideration of the good and pleasant services the king has received from him in the past and for those he hopes still to receive. "

Once installed at Saint-Germain-en-Laye, Taillevent acquired a plot in the priory N.D. d'Hennebent where he planned to build a chapel and arrange for his tomb. During the Revolution, the priory and its annexes were sold as National Properties. The remains of Taillevent and of his two wives were transferred to the town cemetery. A witness to the desecration of the grave reported that pieces of woolen clothing were still intact. In addition to the urns containing charred remains, skeletons of greyhounds were also found lying at the feet of human skeletons. All the bones were tossed into a common grave. No one took the trouble in later years to recover them, but since July 24, 1814, the tombstone has been preserved in the

Musée at Saint-Germain-en-Laye. Numerous casts of it are in existence.

As for the career of the master cook Tirel, it seems to sum up as follows: 1326, kitchen-boy; 1346, head-cook to Philippe VI of Valois; 1355, head-cook and master of the kitchen to the Duke of Normandy; 1375, head-cook to the king, Charles V; 1381, head-cook and master of the garrisons of France and, from 1392 on, master caterer to the king's kitchens.

WHO WAS THE AUTHOR OF THE " MÉNAGIER DE PARIS " ?

Though the author of the *Viandier* is well known, the author of the *Ménagier de Paris* is equally unknown. It is generally thought that the *Ménagier* was written at the request of Charles VI —or of Isabella of Bavaria—between June 1392 and September 1394. It is not solely a book of recipes, but rather a " guide for young households, " indeed a " treatise on conjugal happiness, " certain pages of which are veritable master-pieces. It is a pity no one has thought of re-publishing it...

There is nothing to prove that the *Ménagier* is the work of a single author. In any case, certain of the recipes appear to have been directly

(1) It stood on the present site of 40 and 42 rue de Paris, at Saint-Germain-en-Laye.

inspired by the *Viandier* (1). On reading the *Viandier*, or the *Ménagier*, one is surprised by the number of different spices called for in each recipe. This custom of over-seasoning food was to be continued until the era of Henri IV.

AGNÈS SOREL, FIRST ROYAL MISTRESS TO ENTERTAIN ROYALLY

French cookery owes much to the demi-mondaines. In this respect Agnès Sorel, la Montespan, la Pompadour and even the delicate Madame de Maintenon, yield nothing to Madame Tallien—"our Lady of Thermidor "—nor to the " famous celebrities " of the last century.

" Sex and food—that's the way to hold a man, " explained Maman Poisson, not without reason, to the future Marquise de Pompadour, who profited royally by that advice.

The first of the celebrated royal mistresses to apply that theory was gentle Agnès Sorel. To attract—and hold—Charles VII, not only did she engage the best cooks of the day, but she herself did not hesitate to go into

(1) As the author — or authors — of the *Ménagier*, the names of Jehan de Fleury, the lawyer Jean Louvenet, the banker Jean La Flamant have been suggested.

the kitchen and tie an apron around her waist. Two of her " creations " have been handed down to posterity: salmi of woodcocks and small timbales.

THANKS TO JACQUES CŒUR WE EAT TURKEY

Individual plates, which had disappeared since the days of the Romans, now began to appear again. In servants' halls, French cooks, conscious of their importance, blessed Taillevent for having given them their first letters of nobility. For state banquets many cooks insisted that the food they prepared be served in silver dishes.

Pork butchers obtained the sole right to sell fresh pork meat. The apricot was introduced into France and rapidly gained favor. It was brought from Armenia into Italy at the beginning of the fifteenth century. Candied fruits from Auvergne were popular, as well as sugared almonds from Verdun and *Gigembrats* (jujubes) from Montpellier. Merchants from Guinea brought us the guinea-hen.

Jacques Cœur, Minister of Finance to Charles VII, fallen into disgrace and retired to Turkey, returned to France with a collection of curiosities— among other things, turkeys, which he planned to raise at his château of Beaumont-en-Gâtinais.

31

RECIPES FROM THE MIDDLE AGES
AND FROM THE LADY OF BEAUTY

SOUPE AU PAIN   BREAD SOUP

First make a cullis of sugar and white wine, ornamented with the yolks of eggs and perfumed with a few drops of rose water. Then toast lightly a few slices of bread, cut rather thick, and toss them into the broth. When they are well saturated, dip them in a bath of hot oil. Then plunge them again into the broth, sprinkle them with sugar and saffron. Serve at once (Taillevent).

BROUET D'ALLEMAGNE   GRUEL FROM GERMANY

Blanche and skin some almonds and crush them. Slice several onions very fine and brown in a little oil. Crush ginger, cinnamon, cloves and a little saffron that has first been moistened in verjuice (vinegar). Mix together and pour into a casserole filled with hot water, add some beaten eggs and let boil (Taillevent).

CANARD AU VIN ROUGE   DUCK IN RED WINE

Toast two slices of white bread on a grill, then put them to soak in some red wine. Meanwhile brown a few chopped onions in a little fat. Pound your bread briskly with a pestle. Add cinnamon, nutmeg, a few cloves, sugar and salt. Let all simmer together. Roast the duck until done, add to the bread mixture and finish cooking until meat is very tender.

GALIMAFRÉE   GALLIMAUFRY (HASH)

Take a leg of mutton that you have cooked until medium done. Chop it as finely as possible and mix with minced onions. Stew these ingredients with a little verjuice, butter and ginger. Salt to taste (Taillevent).

MORTEREL   MORTEREL

A kind of hash made with pheasant's meat, kid's leg and bound with eggs (Taillevent).

BROUET D'ANGUILLES   EEL GRUEL

Skin an eel and cut it in very small pieces. Put over a low flame in a casserole in which some good oil is simmering. Salt it and let it cook while you crush with a pestle some ginger and cinnamon, clove, garingal, pepper and saffron. Add this mixture and a bottle of wine to the casserole. Let boil a little (Ménagier de Paris).

CONFITURES DE NOIX

PRESERVED NUTS

*Before St. John's eve gather some fresh nuts. Peel them and make a hole in the middle. Let them soak for nine days, changing the water every day. Dry them thoroughly. Place a clove and a piece of ginger in each hole, put in a pot and cover with honey. The honey must cover the nuts entirely. Three months later it will be ready to eat (*Ménagier de Paris*).*

SALMIS DE BÉCASSES AGNÈS SOREL

SALMI OF WOODCOCK AGNÈS SOREL

1. *When your woodcocks are plucked and singed, split them from the rear to clean them. Remove the gizzard and place everything back inside.* 2. *Lard each woodcock with pork-fat and place in a casserole with the usual seasonings, onions and two glasses of good broth. Let them cook.* 3. *When cooked, remove the woodcocks, take out their intestines. Meanwhile you have prepared a slice of toasted bread which you have spread, while still hot, with a thick layer of foie gras. Sprinkle it with pepper and grated lemon peel. On this "bed" spread the entrails and pour the juice from the casserole over it. Place the woodcock on the croutons and serve hot (Authentic recipe).*

PETITES TIMBALES AGNÈS SOREL

SMALL TIMBALES AGNÈS SOREL

Butter a dozen little molds. Sprinkle them inside with one-half chopped truffles and one-half cooked scarlet (pickled) tongue also finely chopped.

Prepare one pound of creamed chicken forcemeat; finish this off with a few spoonfuls of puréed onions mixed with rice. Fill the molds with this forcemeat, taking care to keep it rather thick and to leave a hole in the middle. Fill this hole with a salpicon made of chicken and truffles bound with Espagnole sauce made with Madeira.

Close the tops of the molds with a heavy layer of wax. Set the molds in a saucepan and pour in hot water half way up the molds. Poach it 15 to 20 minutes near the front of the oven. When ready to serve, unmold, arrange the timbales on the plate on a thin layer of poached forcemeat. Mask the forcemeat with a little Espagnole sauce cooked with the trimmings and liquor of the truffles (Old recipe).

LIÈVRE A LA TAILLEVENT

HARE A LA TAILLEVENT

*Skin and clean your hare, put it on the spit or on a broiler and roast it well. Cut it up and add to it some diced pork-fat. Place all in a good sized pot with some croutons of toasted bread. Pour over this a little beef broth and some wine. Add a little ginger, cinnamon, clove and a pinch of pepper and let it boil (*Viandier*).*

FORMAL FEAST, WITH PEACOCK SERVED ON THE TABLE,
AT LYON IN 1517 *(Photo Josse Lalance)*

Third Course

THE FABULOUS ERA OF CATHERINE DE' MEDICI

One of the greatest dates in the history of French cooking—the greatest of all, perhaps—is October 20, 1553. On that day a very young Italian princess made her appearance at the Court of France: Catherine de' Medici was married to the future Henri II. That event marked the triumph of the Italian Renaissance which had at last succeeded in infiltrating France, bringing in its train a renewal of Arts and Letters. What did it matter that the princess was extremely young (a mere 14 years old)... With her she brought marvelous novelties that were to conquer the French aristocracy completely and captivate the masses.

François I had been reigning for eighteen years. A tremendous eater and a heavy drinker, the King had revived the days of gourmandise and endless drinking-bouts; but those feasts were medieval in character.

Since the time of Louis XI, the court ladies had ceased to share the sovereign's table or the tables of their lords. They claimed that " the movement of the jaws deformed the contours of their face and detracted from the ethereal appeal of their beauty. " They lived on broths which they consumed in the privacy of their own apartments.

The transalpine princess, followed by her Italian escort of both sexes and by a battalion of cooks, was to turn that world topsy-turvy. Catherine and her ladies-in-waiting shared the meals of the sovereign and his lords. Thanks to her a Renaissance of the pleasures of the table was ushered in amid a riot of luxury: earthenware from Urbino, dishes enamelled by Bernard Palissy, glass from Venice and silver engraved by Benvenuto Cellini. Lords and ladies wore their finest furbelows for dinner; music and bacchic songs resounded throughout the banquet hall.

FRANÇOIS I LIKES VEAL, HENRI II PREFERS SNAILS

Catherine was a glutton: her preferences ran to cockscombs, kidneys and artichoke hearts. Sometimes she paid cruelly for her greed. " At Mademoiselle de Martigues' wedding, " a chronicler relates irreverently, " the Queen ate so much she ' almost burst. ' "

That was the great era of veal, considered to be the best of all butchered meats. François I adored it: he also feasted on calves' brains, boiled or fried, and on grilled calves' liver, served with a sauce that had a base of pepper, vinegar and sugar.

Eggs were cooked over hot ashes after first being pricked at the large end lest in the cooking the shell should crack and the egg leak away. The snails, which Henri II loved, were removed from their shells and cooked on the spit like kidneys.

This age was the apotheosis of poultry, no longer served with its adornment of feathers or spitting flames, but stuffed with chestnuts and bacon. It was served on platters and surrounded with a crust made of bread, sugar, orange juice, and rose water. Herons, swans, storks and cormorants were still eaten, but the insipid meat of the peacock was by now a thing of the past. And finally, the guinea-hen was preferred to the pheasant.

Game was not eaten until it was well aged. Flesh that was too young was considered indigestible and unhealthy. People ate partridge, but they did not touch the young; they feasted on hares, but did not eat the leveret. There was, however, one exception to this rule: the flesh of old crows was supposed to be poisonous and only young crows were eaten.

Those huge banquets, those tremendous drinking bouts were not just the prerogative of the court and the nobles. The bourgeois and even the masses had learned to enjoy eating.

" The bourgeois take such delight in a variety of meats that at the end of a meal for ten persons there are three and five dozen soiled dishes left in the kitchen, " declares César Debré.

There were no inns in those days and when a man could not entertain guests at home, he rented a palace whose owners were absent. The concierges, who profited by these arrangements, knew what was wanted and furnished everything: tables, plates and servants. Surprisingly enough, a capon, a partridge, a hare, was less expensive when bought already roasted than when bought raw in the markets. The Italian diplomat, Geronimo Lippomano, explains:

" That is because the *rôtisseurs* (meat cooks, or caterers in cooked viands) buy them in great quantities. They therefore get them at a low price and can resell them cheaply... They are satisfied to earn eight to ten *deniers* provided their money circulates and brings them in something every day. "

Fairs and markets grew abundant. Louis XI created new ones and renewed the licenses of seventy others. François I was to establish three times as many.

" Do you want to buy animals on the hoof at the market ? " adds Lippomano, " or some meat ? You can do so at any time and in any place.

" *Rôtisseurs*, pastry-cooks, will get you up a dinner for ten, twenty or thirty persons in less than an hour. The *rôtisseur* gives you the meat, the pastry-cook the pies, tarts, entrées. The cook gives you *gelées*, sauces, ragoûts.

" This art is so advanced in Paris that there are some publicans who will feed you in their homes at any price: for six pence, for three francs, for thirty or sixty francs per person if you desire... But for sixty francs I hope they will give you manna *en potage* and roast phœnix. "

The habit of eating great quantities of food became so general during the Renaissance that, one year when the harvests were poor (1565), Catherine de' Medici decreed that meals should not include more than three courses.

" Three courses !... Only three courses !... What are we coming to ? " the bourgeois railed, raising their arms to the sky. For six months, at family meals, weddings or funerals, the unfortunate bourgeois had to be content with a menu such as:—

First Course: four to six soups, pâtés, fricassées;

Second Course: hochepot, poultry and fish;

Third Course: fruits, cakes, sweets, preserves.

Soups and potages were still popular. On October 30, 1563—a year of famine—five soups were served in the house of Jehan Malavergne, provost of Paris, who was entertaining old friends: the first soup was made of two capons; a second, of four partridges and cabbage; a third of cockscombs and " *bestilles* " (pigeons' kidneys); a fourth of minced capon and finally—a soup of partridges with lentils.

THE BISHOP OF SENS SETS THE FASHION FOR DONKEY MEAT

The basic meat of the poor was salt pork. But on feast days every laborer and every merchant, no matter how poor he might be, insisted upon eating mutton, roebuck and partridge.

" And some fresh butter with the vegetables, " adds an edict of the Bishop of Chartres.

Whale meat was still greatly prized, though less than at the end of the Middle Ages. The bourgeois ate only the tongue of the whale... and left

CENTER-PIECE MOUNTED
ON GILDED SILVER,
XVITH CENTURY
(Photo Josse Lalance)

the rest to the yokels and other destitute persons or tramps. Whale tongue can be roasted and served with an orange sauce. It can also be run under the broiler and served with a highly spiced sauce. Or else it can be salted and allowed to cook in a court bouillon to which you have added onions ornamented with parsley.

François I appointed as Bishop of Sens his former tutor, Chancellor Duprat. The new bishop was an ardent advocate of donkey meat: he raised and fattened asses' foals specially for his own table. Duprat was also the inventor of a table scooped out so as to permit corpulent guests to " settle " their paunches more comfortably. From this era dates the fashion for asses' milk, which lasted until the last century. When François I was ill, he had asses' milk served to him. On the advice of his physicians, the king also consumed great quantities of yogurt, a practice quickly imitated by his courtiers. At every meal during the month of May the king ate garlic crushed into sweet butter. He was convinced that this rustic food would give him strength and good health for the rest of the year.

The vogue for garlic quickly spread beyond the limits of the Court. From the beginning of the reign of Henri II, doctors always carried a few cloves of garlic in their pockets to protect themselves from illnesses and contagious diseases. These doctors advised their patients to eat *anguilles des bois*

(snakes and adders) once or twice a week each spring. " Their flesh, eaten raw or taken in broth, " explains one of the physicians in his memoirs, " purifies the blood and causes one to perspire more freely. "

THE KING DRINKS, BUT FEARS INTOXICATION AND POISON

Asparagus was rare in France. It did not appear on tables until the time of Louis XIV, when La Quintinie had the idea of growing it in " beds. "

The great gastronomes, gourmets and other " guzzlers " of the Renaissance had little liking for vegetables. As an example, in 1549, the City of Paris gave a banquet for fifty in honor of Catherine de' Medici. They served: 30 peacocks, 33 pheasants, 21 swans, 90 cranes, 30 kids, 66 guinea-fowl, 30 capons, 90 pullets in vinegar, 33 tufted herons, 66 boiled chickens, 66 hazel-grouse, 6 pigs, 99 pigeons, 99 turtle doves, 33 hares, 66 rabbits, some wild rabbits, 13 partridges, 99 quail and 13 young pullets. And only 500 asparagus, 3 bushels of peas, 1 bushel of broad beans and 12 dozen artichokes!

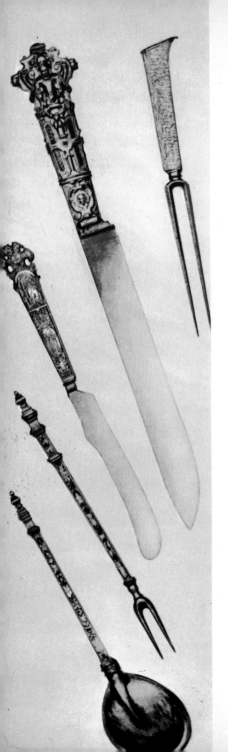

A few years later, at the state banquet honoring the entrance into Paris of Elisabeth of Austria, wife of Charles IX, not one vegetable was served. True, it was Friday, a fast day, and the dinner was limited solely to fish and related food, namely: 1,000 frogs, 200 fresh herring, 200 smoked herring, 10 large turbots, 18 brill, 18 mullets, 50 pounds of whale meat, 18 trout, 50 carp, 15 lampreys, 200 large larval lampreys.

There was little drinking in the Renaissance. People could " eat till they burst, " but it was considered bad form to drink till " one was drunk. " François I like Charlemagne, promulgated a Draconian edict on the subject: his successors were to see that it was strictly carried out. This edict François I drew up in 1536, after learning of the disorders in Brittany caused by people in a state of intoxication.

" Any man convicted of being drunk will be condemned: on the first offense, to detention in prison on bread and water; on the second offense, to be whipped in the inner court of the prison; on the third offense, to be whipped publicly... And on the fourth offense, he shall have both his ears cut off and be banished from the kingdom of France. "

It was not only the fear of intoxication and its resulting follies that made the kings and nobles mistrust

XVITH CENTURY TABLEWARE *(Photo Josse Lalanc*

alcoholic beverages. They were also afraid of poison which, in those days, was often slipped into their cups. Since the Middle Ages, the " princes of the world, " knowing that they were frequently surrounded by hatred, insisted on the " test, " a custom which was to be continued until the days of the Revolution. During the Renaissance, the ceremonial was particularly complicated.

" When the king wished to drink, " reveals the chronicler, César Debré, " the cup-bearer (who was not allowed to leave the table) made a sign to the *sommelier* (wine butler) and to the latter's assistant. Accompanied by guards, the *sommelier* approached, carrying the king's cup and the wine in a flagon; his assistant carried a silver pitcher filled with water.

" The cup-bearer takes the cup and lifts the cover: the *sommelier* pours in the wine and then the water. The cup-bearer fills two silver-gilt cups with some of the diluted wine; he drinks one, the *sommelier* drinks the other... Only then does the cup-bearer hold the glass across the table and he does not remove the cover until the king is about to take it. "

When the king was the guest of one of his subjects, the formalities of the test were incumbent on the host. To dispense with the " proof of the test, " as Henri IV did for Madame de Montpensier, was a mark of great confidence.

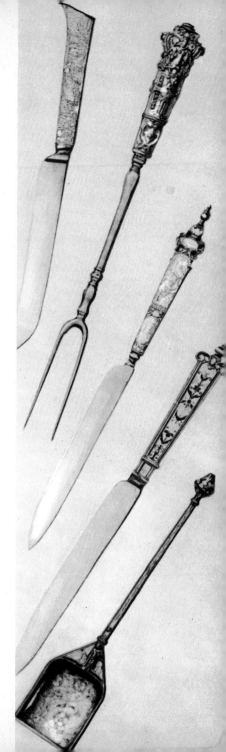

WHAT MONTAIGNE THOUGHT OF COOKS

One of the "revolutions of the table," the most important for the sixteenth century, was the appearance of the fork, made fashionable by Henri III. Its purpose was to prevent spotting the delicate ruff that encircled the necks of gentlemen. Many did not know how to use a fork: people would sharpen them thinking it would make them more practical and they often cut their tongues and lips.

But the use of the fork was slow in gaining general recognition and was not wide-spread until the reign of Louis XVI. For a long time the favorite pastime among the masses and the songwriters of the day was to ridicule that strange implement and the lords and ladies foolish enough to use it. Cooks even advised against it, contending that the fork "spoiled the taste of the food." That the fork remained so long on the black list was due more to their counter-propaganda than to the song-writers' gibes. For, like their successors of later centuries, the great master-cooks of the Renaissance were inclined to take themselves seriously, dispensing aphorisms as if they were the words of the Bible.

Montaigne relates the following conversation he had with one of them.

" He discoursed on that science of cookery with a gravity and a magisterial air as if he were discussing a great point in theology with me.

" He interpreted the differences in appetite: that which one has on an empty stomach, that which one has after the second and the third course; the means to arouse it and to stimulate it; the order of his sauces, at first in general, then describing in detail the qualities of their ingredients and their effects. And all this is in rich and magnificent phrases such as are used to discuss the government of an empire. "

But let us not deride the great cooks of the Renaissance. They left us a thousand recipes and perfected at least as many more.

That age saw the glorification of poultry and of the first dishes of cooked fish. Dessert was king thanks to the marvelous frangipani, the invention of Count Cesare Frangipani. It was presented as a pledge of eternal love to young Catherine de' Medici before she left her native land.

A POET GIVES US A SALAD

No one left a Renaissance table without sampling even the simplest salad: Ronsard describes it for us... The poet's secretary was a charming

GUSTAVE DORÉ

GARGANTUA *(Photo Josse Lalance)*

youth—son of a poet and a poet himself—named Amadys Jamyn. The poet and his secretary are searching for herbs. Ronsard advises Jamyn to look for " lamb's lettuce, the daisy with slender leaf, the bloodwort, so good for the blood and for the spleen and for pain in the side. " He himself will gather the sweet-rooted rampion and the buds of the new currant bushes, the first to appear in Spring. Then reading Ovid, " those beautiful verses in which love is guide, " they will wander slowly back to their dwelling. There, rolling up their sleeves, they will wash their herbs in the waters of his beautiful fountain, blanche them with salt, sprinkle them with rose vinegar, and anoint them with oil from Provence. " The oil from our orchards of France upsets the stomach and is worth nothing. That, Jamyn, that is my *summum bonum.* "

" *Tu t'en iras, Jamyn, d'une autre part,*
Chercher soigneux la boursette touffue

La pasquerette à la feuille menue,
La pimprenelle heureuse pour le sang,
Et pour la ratte, et pour le mal de flanc ;
Je cueilleray, compagne de la mousse
La responsette à la racine douce
Et le bouton des nouveaux groiseliers
Qui le Printemps annoncent les premiers.
Puis, en lisant l'ingénieux Ovide
En ces beaux vers où d'amour il est guide
Regagnerons le logis pas à pas.

Là, recoursant jusqu'au coude nos bras
Nous laverons nos herbes à main pleine
Au cours sacré de ma belle fontaine ;
La blanchirons de sel en mainte part,
L'arronserons de vinaigre rosart,
L'engresserons de l'huile de Provence :
L'huile qui vient aux oliviers de France
Rompt l'estomac et ne vaut du tout rien.
Voylà, Jamyn, voylà mon souv'rain bien.

(In culinary terms: wash thoroughly under running water, salt. If we do not use pepper no doubt that is only because the poet could not find a world to rhyme with it. Use olive oil only.)

SOME RECIPES FROM THE RENAISSANCE

PINTADE A LA MÉDICIS   GUINEA-HEN A LA MEDICI

1. *Stuff a guinea-hen with half a goose liver, diced, with chopped chestnuts and truffles, and a little fat; lard the thighs and the filets and cook the bird in a well-greased casserole in which you have put a carrot and a chopped onion, not forgetting to add a pinch of thyme. Season it, then sprinkle with three glasses of white wine that is not too dry. Let it simmer. When the wine is well reduced, add a bowl of good broth. Cover the casserole and let it cook one hour.*

2. *Meanwhile stuff several larks with diced foie gras larded with a dash of truffles. Brown them lightly and, ten minutes before serving, add them to the marmite in which you have cooked the guinea-hen.*

CARPE A LA ROYALE   CARP A LA ROYALE

1. *First prepare the fish and lard its flesh with cooked truffles; then lay it on a bed of minced vegetables in an ovenproof dish. Butter it generously, season it wisely, cover it with strips of fat and drench it in red wine. Then put it to cook at a low heat for about twelve minutes.*

2. *Through a sieve strain the juice from the dish and add to it a little roux; then add a few* quenelles *(fish-balls), which you might garnish with slices of truffles. Let it cook very, very slowly.*

CARPE A LA MAISON DE FRANCE

CARP A LA MAISON DE FRANCE

This recipe has been handed down by tradition from the kitchens of the royal household of France.

1. *Lard your fish with pork-fat and truffles and let it cook in a good court-bouillon made with Bordeaux wine.*

2. *In another pot, put some pieces of scalded sweet-breads in a good broth, some* quenelles *of the fish stuffing, a few truffles, some cockscombs and soft roes of carp. Let simmer. Then add it all to your fish when it is cooked, not forgetting a spoonful of sugar.*

ROSSOLIS (LIQUEUR)   ROSA SOLIS (LIQUEUR)

Marinate for five days 8 1/4 ounces of red rose petals, 4 1/4 ounces of orange flowers, 1/3 of an ounce of cinnamon, 1 1/8 ounces of cloves in about 11 quarts of alcohol at 22 degrees. Then distill. Finally add 11 pounds of sugar and 1 ounce of Jasmin alcohol.

Henri iv *(Photo Josse Lalance)*

Fourth Course

HENRI IV
DID NOT INVENT
" CHICKEN-IN-THE-POT "

Popular imagination has preserved little of the reign of Henri IV except the triumph of " chicken in the pot "—very little indeed for such a great reign that ended in a veritable revival of France and originated the idea of the " United Nations " of Europe. Moreover the incident is misinterpreted: if the monarch praised chicken in the pot, it was less with the idea of adding to the cuisine of the masses than to encourage the raising of poultry and the cultivation of market-gardening.

In fact the end of the sixteenth century and the beginning of the seventeenth witnessed in particular the triumph of the cabbage to which everyone attributed marvelous properties. It was said to give milk to wet-nurses; to stop hair from falling out; to sharpen one's sense of smell; to cure a certain illness that Madame Férron, with the help of François I, bestowed on the good people of France.

A heavy drinker Henri IV certainly was, but he owed his love of wine— which he never carried to excess—to that Jurançon with which his mother moistened his lips *even before he knew the taste of milk.*

With Henri sumptuous Court repasts and spectacular banquets disappeared for a time. However the use of table linen became general, the cloth being changed during the meal and the napkins after each course. There was one innovation: the guests tied their napkins around their necks; for more than a century before they had flung them over one shoulder or over the left arm. This change—like the innovation of the fork—resulted from the fashion for fluted linen collars which the wearers wished to protect. Because of those ruffs, every man also had to let his neighbor help him tie his napkin around his neck (whence the expression " help to make both ends meet ").

To give a great banquet a man had to be rich and Henri IV was not rich at all. In his memoirs, the Duc d'Angoulême stressed the fact that the king's table was frequently " lacking." And that more than once Henri was obliged to take his meals at the house of one of his lords.

Among the lords, the Marquis d'O... was the most lavish of hosts. Secretary of Finances and a brazen thief, he entertained his master on the revenues of the State. He ground down the people with taxes while he led a life of extreme luxury.

Henri IV much preferred sweets to " chicken in the pot ". His pockets were always full of the bonbons he adored and he offered them to all and sundry. They were those cream bonbons, first made in the reign of Saint-Louis and Philippe-le-Bel when return-ing Crusaders brought sugar from the Orient. From the Renaissance on, those candies were eaten in great quantities.

THANK YOU, MONSIEUR SERRES

Let us go back to the chicken in the pot.

French cooking in general, and the people's pot in particular, owe a debt to Olivier de Serres (1539-1619) rather than to the Béarnais king. Serres was the greatest adventurer—in the noblest sense of the word—in the sixteenth century... and we know what French cuisine owes to courtesans and adventurers.

When he was only nineteen, this staunch " heretic " with the keen eye, generous smiling mouth, thin, aquiline nose, shaved head and short pointed beard, bought a delapidated farm in the Vivarais. Through craftiness, experimentation and hard work, he made it not only the richest agricultural plant in France, but also the field of the most important innovations in market-gardening in all of Europe.

Olivier de Serres occupies an authoritative and important place in the history of French cooking. Thanks to that prodigious magician, beautiful, fresh vegetables were at last to find their place in the most honored casseroles. Since the days of Charlemagne and his timid attempts at garden acclimation, vegetables had been virtually forgotten.

Sully was the first to think that Olivier de Serres could be useful in restoring the land and he summoned him to Paris. Serres arrived on horseback, followed by a convoy of asses laden with sweet-smelling plants and the most beautiful specimens of the vegetables harvested on his estate at Pradel. Before he would enter Sully's presence however, he insisted that the lackeys transfer everything from his convoy to the Prime Minister's office. Sully was enchanted—and so was the king.

Henri IV urged Serres to let his contemporaries profit from his experiments. Serres agreed. He published, one after the other, two remarkable books which mark an epoch in that field: *Théatre de l'Agriculture* and *Mesnage des Champs* (1600). His book is divided into eight parts: the house, cereals, meat, wine and other beverages, garden and orchard, water and wood, ending with sundry advice as to lighting, furniture, clothing and pharmaceutics.

Olivier de Serres was the first in France to praise publicly the advantages of a new species of edible plant: the potato. The potato had been imported into Spain by the *conquistadors*, who,

in 1534, had discovered it in the Andes. At first it was widely distributed in Italy and in Spain. In Austria the botanist, Carolus Clusius, praised its nourishing qualities. No one listened to him and instead people cultivated the potato as an ornamental plant. The fashion reached Berlin in 1651: the flower-beds in the Lustgarten were stocked with them and gentlemen sported the flowers in their buttonholes. England adopted the potato in 1585. France was the last, with Parmentier, in 1769.

SERRES ENCOURAGED THE PEASANTS TO STAY HOME

Nineteen editions of the works of Olivier de Serres were sold. They became the rage among impoverished noblemen, who resolved to put into practice the " return to the soil, " and among families owning landed estates who, after the havoc caused by the religious wars, were planning to give up their fields and settle in the city. It was Serres who uttered that famous phrase to Sully: " Ploughing and grazing are the two breasts of France. "

The incentive had been established. Country gentlemen did not limit themselves to kitchen gardens and market gardens. Many tackled vineyards, buying for exploitation the famous

51

MARDI GRAS *(Photo Josse Lalance)*

vineyards that the abbeys had allowed to remain undeveloped out of discouragement and ignorance. When, as an accompaniment to one of those marvelous " chickens in the pot, " garnished to perfection with fresh, healthy vegetables, you raise a glass of *Clos Vougeot* or of *Chambertin* to your lips... spare a kindly thought for Olivier de Serres. He well deserves it.

52

TWO RECIPES FOR GOOD KING HENRI'S CHICKEN-IN-THE-POT

As for the famous chicken in the pot let us make it together... Here is the traditional, not to say authentic, recipe as discovered and transcribed by Adolphe Brisson.

1. In an earthenware pot put four or five quarts of water and all the vegetables that would go in a *pot-au-feu*.

2. Have a plump chicken and a pound of ham. Take the liver, the heart and the gizzard of your chicken, 1 cup of toasted bread crumbs, 6 ½ ounces of the ham, two or three sprigs of parsley and tarragon, a clove of garlic. Chop all together and put in a dish into which you will break two fresh eggs. Mix all together: season generously with salt, pepper and spices.

3. Stuff the chicken with this force-meat; truss it tightly and put it in the pot as soon as the broth is boiling.

4. Let it simmer over a slow fire for three hours, but do not add the ham until the end of the second hour, so that it will not be overcooked.

Curnonsky discovered another reccipe, also from the same era:—

1. Put 2 - 2 ½ pounds of shin of beef to cook in a court-bouillon with three calf's feet, two chopped carrots, a chopped onion, thyme, bay-leaf, spices.

2. While this is boiling, cut up two chickens and put the pieces of chicken to soak in a good dry white wine with all the condiments for a marinade.

3. When the shin of beef and the calf's feet are cooked, remove them. Strain the court-bouillon and add to it the marinade which you will also

have strained. Put your chickens into this and allow to boil gently.

4. Next, make a white roux with the water in which the chickens were cooked. Add a good portion of cream, about 9 oz. of mushrooms, twenty small onions *sautéd* beforehand in butter and the veal feet boned and cut into pieces. Serve boiling hot. Garnish the chickens with small rounds or slices of good sausage which you have cooked at the same time as the chickens.

LAVARENNE, COOK AND CONFIDENTIAL AGENT

If Henri IV had only a mediocre appreciation of cooking, he liked cooks. He made the fortune of one of them, François-Pierre de Lavarenne, whom he appointed Minister of State.

Lavarenne began as a kitchen-boy in the household of the Duchesse de Bar, sister of Henri IV. It was there that the king noticed Lavarenne, took a fancy to him and trusted him enough to make him his private emissary in many a gallant affair among the ladies of the Court.

It is not known if it was Lavarenne who conducted the negotiations between the king, on the one hand, and the father and the natural brother of charming Henriette d'Entraygues whose virginity had been...sullied. If so, the cook proved to be a wretched diplomat: the king had to pay the two men 10, 000 gold *écus*...for damage and interest. It was rumored, in any case, that the ex-cook did not hesitate to take an important percentage on those " little matters " he handled in the name of his royal client. A chronicler relates that, on meeting her former kitchen-boy in later years, the Duchesse de Bar exclaimed:

" Lucky Lavarenne... You have earned more carrying my brother's " poulets " (literally, chickens; figuratively, love-letters) than you did larding mine. "

Lavarenne, however, had great culinary talents. To him we owe the first books on pastries and cooking clearly edited. Those volumes met with such success that later on, other authors, in particular Nicolas de Bonnefons, used them as a guide.

The best known of François de Lavarenne's books is *Le cuisinier François* (1651). Some people have translated François as Français (French): however, when Lavarenne spoke of himself in his writings—and he was never loath to do so—he always said " the cook François. " Another one of his books—we quote from memory—was *L'École des*

ragoûts, printed in Lyon by Jacques Ganier in 1625, but it is not available today.

From Catherine de' Medici's day it had become customary to spice certain dishes with the effluvia from a glass of liquor. These fumes were said to " kill the worm (*le ver*), " an expression dating from the death of a certain demoiselle de Vernade on whom an autopsy had been performed. During the autopsy, physicians discovered an enormous tapeworm that no poison could kill. It finally died after they had poured a drop of Rosa solis on its head (a liqueur for which we gave the recipe in the preceding chapter).

During the reign of Henri IV, the French lost the habit of drinking wine. Vineyards had been more or less abandoned during the last wars and it was not until the reign of Louis XIII that the advice of Olivier de Serres was to bear fruit again. Consequently wine was expensive and extremely mediocre in quality and people gave up drinking it in preference for herbed wines, spiced wines, aromatic wines. They even went back to hypocras, for which we give here another recipe.

Take one pound of sugar, a little ginger and one ounce of powdered cinnamon. Let it steep for seven or eight hours in three bottles of excellent white wine. Strain six or seven times through a fine sieve.

On feast days, people also drank beer, which they salted in the eastern provinces and to which they added a few

ABRAHAM BOSSE

LA PATISSERIE

bay leaves, gentian bitters or sage in the nothern provinces. (Some people added lavender, not to mention honey.) And then there is the famous punch to which the English Admiral Sir Edward Kennel gave its letters patent. " On October 25, 1599, Sir Edward Kennel, Commander-in-Chief of British Naval forces, offered his ship's company a mammoth punch which he had prepared in a huge marble basin on his estate. He used 80 casks of brandy, 9 of water, 20,000 large limes, 80 pints of lemon juice, 13 quintals (1,300 pounds) of Lisbon sugar, 5 pounds of nutmeg and a huge cask of Malaga wine.

" A platform had been built over the basin to shield it from the rain and the famous beverage was served by a ship's boy who rowed around on the sea of punch in a rosewood boat. To serve the 6,000 guests one ship's boy had to be replaced by another over and over, each boy becoming intoxicated by the fumes from that lake of alcohol at the end of a quarter of an hour. "

The death of Henri IV marks the end of highly spiced cooking, as a comparison of Taillevent's *Le Viandier* with Lavarenne's *Le cuisinier François* proves. French taste became finer, thanks in large measure to Olivier de Serres' " vegetable " discoveries. And also—paradoxically enough—an increase in international business relations had caused the price of spices to drop. No longer a luxury, spices were less in demand.

THE TECHNIQUE
OF BOILING AN EGG

Marie de' Medici—Mme Henri IV— would have no place in a history of French cooking if she had not had among her ladies-in-waiting the charming Princesse de Conti, daughter of the Duc de Guise, who for a brief period was the object of the affections of Henri IV, le Vert-Galant. In her desire to keep the king's favor, the young woman created—perhaps with the aid of Saupiquet, master-cook of the Baron de la Vieuville and the real creator of *pâte feuilletée* (puff paste)— the extraordinary *Carré de mouton à la Conti* (rib of mutton *à la Conti*.)

Nor can we leave Marie de' Medici without speaking of the Cardinal de Richelieu whom she introduced to the Court and whose dupe she ultimately was to become. We mention him briefly here in order not to confuse him later on with the Maréchal de Richelieu whose mayonnaise sauce and banquet of beef will soon be part of our " dramatis personae. "

The Cardinal de Richelieu was the first to serve eggplant, a native product of India, at a state banquet. Gossip holds that he regularly ate *chocolat des affligés*, lozenges of ambergris, which sailors brought him from the Far East and to which the man of the Church attributed aphrodisiac properties.

But the Cardinal was no great gourmet. From the age of 25, he was never without a day's illness: fevers, liver attacks, neuralgia, hemorrhoids, boils, bladder troubles, abscesses as painful as they were humiliating.

Before we start on the *Grand Siècle*, let us devote a few lines to Louis XIII. Louis XIII had a favorite pastime: he liked to cook. Unfortunately he has not left us any culinary treatise. His specialties, in which he excelled, lay in making jams and in cooking eggs " a hundred different ways. "

56

It was in this era that Nicolas de Bonnefons gave us his famous *Technique des œufs à la coque* :

" Everyone has his own way of boiling eggs: one cook will put them on the stove in a pot filled with cold water and remove them the moment the water boils. Another will have the water boiling before he puts in the eggs, and then count quickly up to two hundred before taking them out.

" These two methods are far from perfect: they merely seal the white and leave the yolk uncooked.

" If you take my advice, you will put two pints of water in an earthenware casserole and when the water begins to bubble, put in your eggs. At the same time take the pan off the fire and put it aside. When the water has cooled to the point where you can plunge in your hand without burning yourself, take out your eggs. They are done. "

(Photo Josse Lalance)

57

LOUIS XIII AT LUNCHEON

(Photo Josse Lalance)

RECIPES OF A *VERT-GALANT*

CIVET DE LIÈVRE LAVARENNE   JUGGED HARE LAVARENNE

Take a hare and cut it in pieces. Put the pieces in a pot with some broth seasoned with a bouquet garni and cook them thoroughly. When the hare is half cooked, add a little wine and thicken with a little flour. Add an onion and a little vinegar. Serve with a green sauce.

SAUCE VERTE   GREEN SAUCE

Take some green corn. Toast a slice of bread which you have dipped in vinegar, pepper and salt. Add the corn, crush all together and strain through a cloth (Lavarenne).

(This recipe was valid in a day when hunting was not regulated. Now at the season when the corn is green, it is difficult to procure a hare.)

PERDRIX A L'ESTOUFFADE   STEWED PARTRIDGE

Lard your partridges with fat bacon. Put them in a skillet with a little butter and some melted pork fat. When they are nicely browned, cover them with good, highly seasoned broth and let them cook. To garnish, take some truffles, mushrooms and fricasséed asparagus. Simmer all together. Serve with lemon and pistachio nuts. If the sauce is not thick enough, add a little flour, but it should not be too thick (Lavarenne).

CARRÉ DE MOUTON A LA CONTI   RIB OF MUTTON A LA CONTI

Prepare a rib of mutton by removing the skin which is found on the fillet (loin). Take a quarter of a pound of bacon fat generously larded with chopped anchovies mixed with pepper, two shallots and a little parsley. Chop a bay leaf, four leaves of basil and some tarragon leaves very, very fine. Lard the skinned meat with the pork fat and anchovies; put it in a casserole, moisten with a glass of white wine and a glass of broth. Add your minced herbs.

Skim the grease off the sauce and add butter the size of a walnut molded with a little flour. Heat the sauce, let it thicken on the stove and pour over the meat.

LA BÉARNAISE   BEARNAISE

Contrary to what is generally supposed, sauce béarnaise does not date from the time of Henri IV. It seems to owe its name to the fact that it was made for the first time, in the last century, at the Pavillon Henri IV, in Saint-Germain-en-Laye.

CHOU FARCI VERT-GALANT   STUFFED CABBAGE VERT-GALANT

Half a century ago, Fulbert Dumonteil announced that he had found the following recipe from the days of Henri IV.

1. Parboil your cabbage. Remove it carefully from the pot and drain it thoroughly. Open it, leaf by leaf, using the greatest care. It was dome-shaped, it now becomes a rosette.

2. While the cabbage is cooking, you have had time to prepare an excellent stuffing of sausage meat, chicken livers and bread crumbs which you have bound with the yolk of one egg and seasoned according to taste.

3. Spread each leaf with your stuffing. Then, with a light hand, gently bring the leaves back towards the heart of the cabbage which you have filled with finely minced chicken livers.

4. The cabbage is now in normal shape again. Tie it gently and place it lovingly in a large casserole in which a light roux (in which you have put several cloves of cinnamon) is simmering. Let it cook till done. When ready to serve, scatter a few capers over the stuffing and moisten with a small glass of excellent alcohol.

CARBONADE   BEEF SOUP

Cut several pieces of beef in slivers which you sauté in fat with a lot of onions. Moisten it with wine and cover with slices of bread spread with a thick layer of mustard. When the meat is done, add a trickle of vinegar, a little sugar and a good tomato sauce.

LE DINÉ DV ROY A L'HOTEL DE VILLE DE PARIS

Fifth Course

LOUIS XIV, THE MOST ILLUSTRIOUS GLUTTON

The age of Louis XIV!

The teachings of Olivier de Serres now bore fruit. Gastronomical customs and culinary recipes appeared in new forms that were very close to our own of today. Food supplies continued to increase. Market-gardens and kitchen-gardens under cultivation flourished. Vineyards produced the finest wine: people were now able to drink it without flavoring it. Good food became an art. More and more cook books appeared. In one of them the famous chef, L.B. Robert, wrote:

" Pyramids of meats and heavily spiced broths and thick soups are no longer to our taste. Today we prefer an exquisite selection of meats which each guest is served separately, the finesse of their seasoning, the courtesy and cleanliness of each course. "

Bonnefons, one of Louis XIV's lackeys, published *Les Délices de la campagne* (1655), which presents in the clearest terms the best preparations " for the delights of life and of everything that grows on the land and in the waters. "

M. de Bonnefons had an entrée almost everywhere, among the great as well as those of lesser importance. He had a keen eye and his book is full of instructive information. In the chapter on arranging a formal dinner we read, for instance:

" The great fashion is to place four fine soups at the four corners of the table with four dish stands between each two, with four salt cellars placed near the soup tureen.

" On the dish stands are placed four entrées, in low pie dishes. Guests' plates should be deep so that they can use them for the soup or for helping themselves to whatever they wish to eat without taking it spoonful by spoonful out of the serving dish as they might be disgusted at the sight of a spoon which had been in the mouth of a person, being dipped into the serving dish without being wiped.

" The second course will consist of four substantial dishes set in the corners, either a court-bouillon, a piece of beef or a large roast, and salad on the plates. The third course will consist of roast poultry and game, small roasts and all the rest. The middle of the table is left free as otherwise the head steward will have difficulty in reaching across it, because of its great size. If desired, fill the centre of the table with melons, various salads in bowls or on little plates to make serving them easier, oranges and lemons. Preserves in syrup on marzipan biscuits could also be put there. "

64

THANKS TO COFFEE, BUSINESS FLOURISHES IN MARSEILLE

The Sun King was a glutton. He ate without discernment, and he ate enormously. He would think nothing of four huge plates of different kinds of soup, a whole pheasant, a partridge, vegetables, a large dish of salad, two big slices of ham, mutton with garlic, a plate of cakes and—to wind up a good meal—eggs prepared in various ways.

Thanks to the Sun King, oysters regained the popularity they had lost since the days of the Romans (Louis never ate less than a hundred), although certain physicians attributed numerous ills to them. For the first time people thought of cooking them.

Families no longer ate in their bedrooms or in the halls of their dwellings. Every respectable household now boasted a dining room. Among the bourgeoisie, the mistress of the house had become aware of the importance of her role. She knew how to order meals and she strained her ingenuity to show off her good taste.

The national dish was the *pot-à-oie*—it was to remain popular right up to the Revolution. The recipe is simple: take an enormous goose and stuff it with various meats, especially feathered game (pheasants, quail, woodcock, pigeons, ortolans, etc.). Place a few aromatic herbs inside the poultry as well. Put it in the oven to

LES PLAISIRS DE LA VIE

L'ODORAT   L'OUYE   LE GOUST   LA VEUE   L'ATTOUCHEMENT

THE PLEASURES OF LIFE *(Photo Josse Lalance)*

roast. The most refined persons ate only the stuffing: they left the goose for the servants, yokels and the poor.

Coffee appeared in France under Louis XIV. The king drank it for the first time in 1644 when merchants from Marseille presented it to him. To thank them, the king decreed that henceforth all coffee to enter the realm must be unloaded exclusively at the port of Marseilles. However, coffee did not became popular until around 1669. In Paris at that time, the Turkish ambassador to France was the first to offer it to visitors who called on him. But a year later, in the neighborhood of the Palais Royal, young men were to be found going from door to door selling a cup of coffee for two *sous*, sugar included.

65

From coffee to cafés was but a step. In 1672, an Armenian at the Saint-Germain fair opened the first shop where one could sample coffee " on the spot. " The man made a fortune. He soon had many imitators. Those first cafés were in fact veritable smoking-rooms where travelers who had lived in the Orient and knights of Malta gathered. Fifteen years later, a certain Widow Fournier took over a café on the rue Saint-Antoine. She was the first to provide her regular customers with newspapers to read. Not to be outdone, the owner of the Café des Grâces, rue de l'Arbre-Sec, installed the first public billiard table; the Café de la Régence became the recognized rendez-vous for chess players.

DOM PÉRIGNON, ANCESTOR OF PÈRE GAUCHER

Another innovation: vendors of ices.

A Sicilian, Procopio, introduced ices and sherbets into France in 1660. Ten years later he opened the " Café Procope " on the rue des Fossés Saint-Germain. His success was immediate and it inspired so many imitators that he was soon obliged to draw up rules and regulations for a *Corporation des Glaciers*. There were two hundred and fifty members. Their ices, however, were not good and they made no effort to improve them, though they sold them at a high price. France had to wait another century before ices acquired a taste and became an estimable dessert.

People began to talk of a Benedictine, Dom Pierre Pérignon (1638-1715), in charge of the cellars of the Abbey of Hautvilliers near Epernay. He was said to have discovered the secret of making the wine of Champagne " bubble and sparkle. " However it was impossible to commercialize his discovery: there were no bottles strong enough to contain and carry his new marvel. Certain attempts made in the following century were to prove satisfactory. But the world had to wait almost another half century before English glassblowers perfected bottles of " dark glass " that were thick and strong.

In Budapest, the bakers had saved their city from an invasion by the Turks (1686). Working at night, they heard the attackers digging underground passages and were able to give the alarm. As a reward, they were given the sole right to bake special cakes made in the shape of the crescent, the emblem on the Ottoman flag. Soon Parisian pastrycooks were also baking these " croissants. "

The benefits of tea from China were discovered. On the day of her marriage to Louis XIV, Maria-Thérèsa of Austria, that ill-favored woman who " even has hair between her breasts, " according to Bonnefons, the faithful valet, introduced her royal husband to the taste of chocolate. Soon all the Court was drinking chocolate in great quantities and Madame de Sévigné praised the product " imported into Europe by the Spaniards " — a statement that was violently contradicted by Madame de Grignan.

THE VATEL ENIGMA

Louis XIV paid no attention to those controversies. It is true that he had a phenomenal appetite. On his death his physicians discovered that his stomach was three times larger then a normal stomach. In his intestines lived a tapeworm of record size—it, too, living like a *grand seigneur.*

The king would eat anything: soups, fish, meat, game and even pastries which were coming into their own. On the rue de la Verrerie, the Parisian pastry-cook, Charles-Paul Favart, perfected échaudés, making the dough rise by poaching it in hot water and drying it in the oven. Monthier (the elder), Madame de Maintenon's chef, was the great specialist of the *flamiche.* This *flamiche* was a sort of griddle cake, made of baker's dough, rolled out thin and baked in the oven. Louis XIV ate it very hot, spreading it with thick layers of butter and jam.

With such a monarch, how could his reign fail to be a period of glory for cooks and those men known as " *les coteaux.* " So called because merely by raising a glass of wine to their lips they could tell from which " *coteau* " (hillside) the wine came.

The rapid rise to favor of cooks was not to the liking of all. One chronicler writes:

" We have two kinds of persons in society, doctors and cooks: the former work to preserve our health, the latter to ruin it. The only difference is that the latter are more certain to succeed than the former. "

Was there, among those master-cooks, a man named Vatel? This is a question that is pondered today. Perhaps the Marquise de Sévigné exaggerated the reputation of the man concerned. One fact is certain: there is no document in existence to prove that Vatel was a cook. No book, no recipe he could have written has come down to posterity. *No chronicler of the age, except Madame de Sévigné, ever mentions his name.* She has given us, in her letter of April 24, 1671, the only document relating to Vatel. In it she writes:

" Vatel, the great Vatel, maître d'hôtel to Monsieur Fouquet and recently maître d'hôtel to Monsieur le Prince, stabbed himself... "

There is, therefore, a Vatel enigma. A maître d'hôtel? Perhaps. In any case a shoddy one to prefer to desert in a professionally critical situation and run

a sword through his body rather than face up to the consequences.

We cannot end this brief journey through the kitchens and sculleries of the *Grand Siècle* without mentioning Louis de Béchamel. Béchamel was a financier who became rich through fraudulent deals. His competence allowed him to indulge himself as a gastronome and an amateur cook. However his chief claim to fame was his invention of the sauce that bears his name—and for which he may be forgiven much.

BREAD BECOMES IMPORTANT

Bread was now the basic food of the common people and it was to continue to grow in importance until the war of 1940 when the French were forced to ration it. Brie, the granary of the capital, supplied Paris with half of its wheat. The countryside was dotted with windmills as well as the ovens in which the peasants baked their round loaves. Bakers crowded into the towns, where their profession was strictly regulated. They were allowed in the markets only after the needs of private individuals had been supplied; and even then purchases were limited in quantity to prevent them from piling up clandestine stocks.

The baker was obliged to sell his bread himself—or to have his wife or his children sell it—in order to eliminate middlemen. All bread had to be sold before noon. Until midday the price was open and was determined by bargaining. After midday the price of bread was frozen at the rate reached at noon. After four o'clock, bread had to be sold at a reduced price. The *bête noire* of the bakers was the Royal Pantler, who had full power over them. He had twenty-four lesser pantlers under his orders: honest gentlemen who watched over the sale of bread in all the large cities of the realm, at a wage of 700 livres per month.

In spite of those restrictions, the baker's profession was even then one of the best. A Parisian ate, on an average, one pound of bread per day and country people nearly one pound more. Baking was therefore a profession that brought in a comfortable living, and such a thing as a strike was unknown. To be a baker was, in a way, a stepping stone to the bourgeoisie. However bread was not held in such high esteem at Court as it was in the bosom of the great bourgeois households. The nobility considered it incorrect to serve it on the table. It was as much as saying: " Excuse us! We are too poor to offer you anything else!"

When towards the end of his life Louis XIV lost all his teeth, he resigned himself, though with repugnance, to eating moistened breadcrumbs.

THE COOK *(Photo Josse Lalance)*

SOME RECIPES OF THE *GRAND SIÈCLE*

LES ŒUFS EN MEURETTE   EGGS EN MEURETTE

In a casserole put a glass of wine and half a glass of water, an onion cut in slices, a little garlic, a bay leaf and some parsley. Salt and pepper and let it boil about twenty minutes. Poach four eggs in this sauce. Take them out carefully and place them on a hot dish. Thicken the sauce with some beurre manié, *let it boil a few minutes and pour over the eggs.*

L'OMELETTE AU SUCRE   SUGAR OR DESSERT OMELET

Mix thoroughly the yolks of eggs with some powdered sugar until well blended. Add a tiny pinch of salt. Meanwhile beat the whites to a stiff froth with some grated orange rind. Blend carefully the yolks and the whites and make your omelet as usual. Before serving, sprinkle with sugar and run a hot salamander over it to caramelize it (or run it under the broiler).

TERRINE D'HUITRES   TERRINE OF OYSTERS

1. Line an oven-proof dish with a layer of crust dough. Put it in the oven until the dough is cooked.

2. Melt some butter and add flour to it, stirring all the time. Add an onion and let it cook a few minutes. Add, still stirring, three or four glasses of liquid from the oysters, some thyme, bay leaf, parsley, salt, a little minced garlic and a handful of bread crumbs.

3. Toss in six dozen shelled oysters (for six persons). Mix gently and add a few lumps of butter.

4. Cover with a fairly thin layer of dough, spread it evenly and make an X on it. Put it in the oven and bake until the crust is golden.

COTELETTES A LA MAINTENON   LAMB CHOPS A LA MAINTENON

1. In a frying pan pour a claret glass of Madeira, with a pinch of coarse ground pepper, a few minced mushrooms. Reduce the liquid to three-fourths.

2. Prepare a sauce of half milk, half bouillon : simmer gently and reduce until it thickens enough to permit you to mask the chops with it ; thicken with the yolk of an egg and add a little crushed garlic.

3. Sauté the chops until half done ; arrange them on a platter, spacing them. Cover them with the sauce and finish cooking in a very hot oven until the top is golden. When ready to serve, moisten with a little of liquid no. 1 and send the rest of the sauce to the table in a sauce boat (Ed. Richardin).

CAILLES EN RAGOÛT   QUAIL STEW

Split your quail in half. Let them brown in a casserole with some bacon and a little flour to bind the sauce well. Moisten with some broth; add salt, pepper, fines herbes, minced mushrooms, artichoke hearts. When they are thoroughly cooked, add a small glass of liquor and the juice of an orange or a dash of lemon. (Authentic recipe).

CANETON EN RAGOÛT   DUCK STEW

Roast a duck whole. Meanwhile prepare a ragoût of sweetbreads, artichokes, mushrooms, a bouquet of fines herbes, salt and pepper, which you will cook in the casserole with a little melted fat.

When your ragoût is done and your duck cooked to a turn, pour the ragoût over the duck and add a drop of vinegar (Bonnefons).

MOREAU LE JEUNE

AN EXQUISITE SUPPER *(Photo Josse Lalance)*

Sixth Course

THE "PETITS SOUPERS": WIT BUBBLES IN CASSEROLES AND CHAMPAGNE IN GLASSES

The eighteenth century was by no means the most ignominious era in French history: Louis XIV died having shown the French that it was possible for them to surpass themselves. Historians were to turn, first, against the Regent and then against Louis XV, forgetting that eighteen years of peace would restore the country after sixty years of war. They would forget that the wealth created by industry and distributed by trade was to erase the inequality in fortunes. They would forget that the spirit of conviviality in that era would prevail in every class of French society. And that is what interests us today.

Even in the reign of Louis XIV, the mistress of the house realized the importance of her position. With Louis XV, she prided herself on her activities: interiors became attractive and comfortable; instead of renting a mansion or a palace when he wished to entertain his friends, the master of the house entertained at home. And the honors and thanks fell to his wife.

" Little suppers " for two or three pairs of good friends became fashionable. And in that lay the secret of good food. If it was comparatively easy for a cook getting rid of a lot of obligations to prepare a banquet for a hundred, it was a more delicate matter for the mistress of the house to excite the appetite of four guests with only a couple of dishes.

MEALS ARE SERVED WITH CLOCK-LIKE PRECISION

Under the Regent, and then under Louis XV, a distinct separation was established between gourmandise and gluttony. The word gastronomy was revived from the Greek at this time. Social gatherings became more frequent in all classes of society. Everyone was eager to entertain his friends. This was the age of conversation: wit bubbled in casseroles and champagne in glasses.

Louis XV—the Well-Beloved— was himself a discriminating epicure. He was interested in everything related to the culinary arts. If before him the Sun King had granted several patents (among them the one for the sale of ices, granted to the merchant Louis de Beaumont)—his great-grandson, in order to encourage competition, granted a multitude of others.

The king's wife, Marie Leczinska, and his favorites competed fiercely to present him with choice dishes. And, following the example of the Queen and her courtiers, ladies of the aristocracy were not shy about giving their names to dishes they had invented, or even to those they merely liked. Sometimes they went so far as to purchase the inventions of some chef of genius and retitle his recipes with their own names. Such was the case with *Côtelette à la (princesse de) Soubise* and *Gigot à la (duchesse de) Mailly*.

At Marie Leczinska's table, Louis would be served *Bouchées à la reine* (Vol au vent of chicken), *Poulet à la reine* (Chicken *à la reine*), sometimes followed by *consommé à la reine*. For these three dishes we are indebted to Vincent de la Chapelle, master-cook of the French royal household, who also invented *Filet d'aloyau braisé à la royale* (Filet of sirloin braised *à la royale*.)

However, to the Queen's dining room, Louis preferred the intimate little dinners of his favorites; those of la Du Barry and of la Pompadour in particular, where *petits soupers* were served with exquisite taste and luxury. Everything was presented with the clock-like precision of automatons. After each course the table disappeared through an opening in the floor, descending to the floor below where it was cleared, then quickly set again before being raised.

" Thus, they say, guests are not annoyed by the importunate glances of servants. They are freed of all embarrassment and need not blush on being caught unawares. "

NÉE

Murmurs at supper *(Photo Giraudon)*

COURTIERS,
BOTH MEN AND WOMEN,
TAKE TO THE KITCHEN

At Madame Du Barry's the master of the ovens was Mauconseil thanks to whom we have the famous recipe for Partridge in Chartreuse (*Perdrix en chartreuse*). Mauconseil advised the sovereign to eat " *animelles* " (ram's testicles), which Louis XV conceded to have marvelous qualities.

At la Pompadour's, Monthier-the-Younger officiated in the kitchens. He was the son of Monthier-the-Elder, whom we saw in the service of Madame de Maintenon. Monthier-the-Elder was the son of Old Monthier who presided over the kitchens of the House of Condé. With such a mastercook, the Marquise de Pompadour was to have an opportunity to attach her name to several dishes we still enjoy today.

To gain the King's good graces, the courtiers, in their turn, took to the kitchen. Each one wanted to have either a dish named for him or a speciality that was served only at his table. Villeroy—the only Maréchal de France who never won a battle—gave to culinary science a sauce in which the mashed yolks of hard-boiled eggs are bound with butter. This preparation was served at his table with pieces of chicken, cooked in well-seasoned broth, then strained. The chicken was coated thoroughly with the sauce, rolled in breadcrumbs, and then plunged into hot fat (*Poulet à la Villeroy*).

Mirepoix, who was also to die in bed as a Maréchal de France, insisted on nothing but the best from his mastercooks. To them we owe the quail cooked in Xérès wine (*Cailles à la Mirepoix*), and also a sauce (*à la Mirepoix*) which is still one of the classics of cooking.

Cardinal de Bernis, who shared with Louis XV the favors of Madame de Pompadour, invented *crêpes dentelles*.

None of them, however, could equal the Duc de Richelieu (1696-1788). Adventurer and sybarite, a tremendous eater and a discriminating gourmet, a dissolute rake and a man of honor, this second cousin of the Cardinal was at once a gay Lothario, *un homme à femmes*, and *un homme de cuisine*. It was at his table, that mahonnaise— now mayonnaise—was served for the first time after the capture of Port-Mahon in 1759. He was also the author of the famous " meal of beef " which he offered to the princes and princesses taken prisoner by his troops during the Hanoverian war. Strange as it may seem, this menu is perfectly orthodox: it obeys all the rules concerning the organization of meals which were in force at that period.

Here it is as Président Hénault reports it in his memoirs:

" My Lord, " said Rullière, the Duc's aide-de-camp, much disturbed on learning that the Duc de Richelieu wanted to give a supper to a number of guests, " there is nothing in the kitchens except a carcass of beef and a few roots... "

" Very good! " said the Maréchal, " That is more than one needs to provide the prettiest supper in the world. "

" But, my lord, it would be impossible... "?

" Come, Rullière, calm yourself and write down the menu I will dictate to you. "

Seeing Rullière more and more alarmed, the Maréchal took the pen out of his hand and sitting down at his secretary's desk, wrote the following " menu for a supper. "

Centerpiece: The large silver platter with the equestrian statue of the King, and the figures of Du Guesclin, Dunois, Bayard, Turenne. The silver plate with my coat-of-arms embossed and enamelled on it.

First Course: a tureen of *garbure gratinée*, made of beef consommé.

Four hors-d'œuvre: Palate of our beef *à la Sainte-Menehoulde*. Pâtés of chopped fillet of beef with chives. Beef kidneys with fried onions. Tripe *à la poulette* with lemon juice.

To follow the soup: Rump of beef garnished with root vegetables in gravy (because of the Germans trim these vegetables into grotesque shapes).

Six entrées: Oxtail with a purée of chestnut. Civet of tongue (*à la bourguignonne*). *Paupiettes* of beef *à*

l'estouffade with pickled nasturtium buds. Fillet of beef braised with celery. Beef rissoles with hazel-nut purée. Beef marrow on toast (ration bread will do).

Second course: Roast sirloin (baste it with melted marrow). Endive salad with ox-tongue. Beef *à la mode* with white jelly mixed with pistachio nuts. Cold beef with blood and Jurançon wine. (Don't make a mistake!)

Six final dishes: Glazed turnips with the gravy of the roast. Beef bone marrow pie with bread crumbs and candy sugar. Beef stock aspic with lemon rind and pralines. Purée of artichoke hearts with beef gravy and almond milk. Fritters of beef brain steeped in Seville orange juice. Beef gelée with Alicante wine and Verdun mirabelles... And then, all that is left in the way of jams and preserves.

(*Note:* if by any unfortunate chance, this meal turns out not to be very good, I shall withhold from the wages of Maret (the master-chef) a fine of 100 *pistoles*... Now go and stop worrying!) (*Signed: Richelieu*).

Président Hénault (1685-1770), who preserved this " historic " menu for us, was the Superintendant of the Queen's household. His fame, however derives much more from the fact that he presided over the salon of Madame Du Deffand (1697-1780) where Fontenelle, Voltaire, Montesquieu, d'Alembert, Hume and the Duchesse de Choiseul would gather. Here every man did his utmost to shine, each trying to

A PAUSE IN THE HUNT *(Photo Josse Lalance)*

win the favors of his hostess who, actually, hardly ever granted them. From time to time she would signal to a lackey, who would pass the guests *baraquilles* (a hot hors-d'œuvre)— today they would be called " zakuskis" —with various garnishes. Some of them were spread with " kavia "— the caviar which Rabelais had mentioned in his *Pantagruel* and which had come back in fashion—or more simply with *boutargue*, a preparation made from the roe of grey mullet, dried and mashed.

It was in one of those salons that there was talk, for the first time in Paris, of a new cheese, the formula for which a Norman peasant, Marie Marel, had perfected in her village of Camembert (1781).

Gastronomy was the fashion even in the salons.

A story went the rounds about the Maréchal de Luxembourg who, having missed his dinner hour, ordered his servants to bring him only one of the dishes they had prepared. His chef, caught unawares, presented him with a cold fricassée of chicken jellied in its pale sauce. The Maréchal tasted it and was delighted: he had just discovered *Chaud-froid de volaille.*

A FEW RECIPES FOR "LITTLE SUPPERS"

FILET D'ALOYAU BRAISÉ A LA ROYALE
BRAISED SIRLOIN A LA ROYALE

Remove the fillets of the joint and cut off all the fat, taking care to tie them carefully so they will retain the best shape for serving either on an oval dish or on a round dish.

In the bottom of a large casserole put some slices of bacon and some slices of veal, five or six onions, several cloves of cinnamon and a bouquet garni. Place the fillet in the casserole, cover with fat and pour 3 cups of excellent broth over it. Let it cook for half an hour over a hot fire, lower the heat and simmer for six hours. Let it cool in the same dish, then reheat, using half the liquid in which it has been cooked. (It can also be served à la gelée if one is careful beforehand to add a calf's foot to the pot with approximately one ounce of hartshorn.)

POULET A LA REINE MARIE LECZINSKA
CHICKEN A LA REINE MARIE LECZINSKA

To season the chicken you will use a seasoning in great honor in Central Europe—paprika. Cut a young chicken up in pieces and dip in fresh water. Meanwhile make a roux with minced onions ; salt it and add a spoonful of paprika and half a glass of thick tomato sauce. Add the pieces of chicken to this mixture, cover and let simmer

for one hour, stirring it several times. Before serving, add a little cream to the sauce, blend well but do not allow it to boil.

KNOCKLES   DUMPLINGS TO GARNISH AND ACCOMPAGNY THE POULET A LA REINE

All you have to do is to put about fifteen spoonfuls of flour in an earthenware pot, add some eggs and mix until the dough no longer sticks. Let the dough rest. Then shape it in the form of a cylinder and cut it in fairly thick rounds. Toss the rounds into salted boiling water and cook for ten minutes.

PERDRIX EN CHARTREUSE A LA DU BARRY
CHARTREUSE OF PARTRIDGE

First cook a partridge in a stewing pan with some fat bacon, diced ham, sliced carrots and minced onions. Season with salt and pepper and add a good white wine with an equal amount of broth. Meanwhile braise some cabbage with a little salt pork and some sausages. Serve the partridge on the braised cabbage, surrounded by salt pork and sausages.

FILETS DE SOLE POMPADOUR   FILLETS OF SOLE POMPADOUR

Take some fillets of sole and spread them on one side with a forcemeat of truffles and chopped mushrooms. Roll the fillets and cook them in champagne, adding a bouquet garni *and the usual seasonings. When ready to serve, arrange on a hot dish, the centre of which is garnished with shelled crayfish tails. Before serving, cover with the sauce.*

Seventh Course

PARMENTIER GIVES FRANCE ITS NATIONAL VEGETABLE

On August 25, 1785 a great reception was held at Versailles to celebrate the birthday of Louis XVI. All the courtiers and important personages in France had been invited. The King appeared to be deeply moved by so many marks of devotion. Suddenly a tall, broad-shouldered man with a big nose and a square, stubborn chin burst through the crowd, holding above his head, to keep it from being crushed in the general hurlyburly, a bouquet of little purple flowers. Reaching the king's side, he bowed and held out the flowers to him.

" Sire, " he said in a voice hoarse with emotion, " I have come to offer you a bouquet worthy of you and I am sure no flowers that will be presented to you today will be more acceptable to your Majesty. "

The king took the bouquet, and looked at it a long time with evident curiosity. Then he smiled.

" Monsieur Parmentier, " he said at last, " men like you are not rewarded by money. There is a currency worthier of their hearts... Give me your hand; and come and embrace the Queen (sic). "

Historic words—and a historic moment. Louis XVI had just given his accolade to the potato and at the same time a new war horse to French cuisine.

LANCRET

HAM AT LUNCHEON *(Photo Giraudon)*

The king did not lay the bouquet aside immediately. For a long time he and the Queen looked first at the flowers and then at Antoine-Auguste Parmentier.

" Sire, " said the latter, " from now on famine is impossible. "

The king held out one of the flowers to Marie-Antoinette who pinned it on her corsage. He himself put a flower in his button-hole. Finally he held out a third flower to Parmentier.

The next morning everyone at Court was eager to sport the potato flower in his buttonhole. Some even paid as high as ten louis for them.

PARMENTIER: A PRISONER WHO DOES NOT COME BACK EMPTY-HANDED

Parmentier was then forty-eight years old. He was born at Montdidier (Somme) on August 12, 1737, on the rue de la Mercerie which today bears his name. An ecclesiastic, who directed his first studies, saw that the young man was interested in pharmacy and placed him, in 1753, as an assistant clerk with the pharmacist Frisson, Place de la Croix-Bleue.

Later on Frisson recommended his assistant to an apothecary of the Palais-Royal, sieur Simonet. The latter directed the young man toward military pharmacy; in 1757 we find Parmentier on the battle-field of the Hanoverian army, under the orders of the celebrated chemist, Bayen.

Parmentier the " apothecary " was made of the stuff of heroes. He was cited for courage and enthusiasm in caring for the wounded under enemy fire. He was even caught five times and stripped by thugs who robbed corpses.

" I do not know, " he wrote after one of these encounters, " any valets as clever as those Prussian Hussars. They disrobed me faster than I could have done myself. They are extremely honest fellows; they did not do me the slightest harm; they took only my clothes and my money. "

But, the sixth time, those " extremely honest fellows " were not satisfied with stripping Parmentier. They took him prisoner. Some weeks later we find our man on damp straw in a German prison.

It was the year 1761. One hundred and thirty years earlier, the potato had been brought to Europe by the Conquistadors. It had come into general use in Italy, Belgium and Germany, but not in France. Olivier de Serres had tried, unsuccessfully, to make it popular, but he did not press the point as he was not sure if the potato was not a cause of leprosy !

PARMENTIER *(Photo Bulloz)*

In Italy, in Belgium and in Germany, people did not throw the tubers away: they fed them to cattle, poor people and...prisoners. For more than a year of captivity, Parmentier lived on potatoes and during that time he conceived the idea of popularizing, in France, the culture of what was rapidly to become the French national vegetable.

His efforts in Paris after his liberation were unsuccessful, but indefatigable propagandist that he was, he stubbornly persisted, to the point where he was severely criticized. In 1769, while Parmentier was a pharmacist at the Hôtel des Invalides, he was the victim of a nasty intrigue in which he was accused of trying to make the pensioners of the Hospice eat potatoes. Parmentier was obliged to hand in his resignation.

Ten years later, the town of Besançon held a competition on the theme: " Plants that can best replace cereals in time of famine. " Parmentier gave a report advocating what he called *solanum tuberosum* (he was never to know it by the word *parmentière*, or potato). He won the first prize. But in Paris, his enemies never lost an opportunity to recall that he had tried to make the glorious army pensioners of the Invalides eat " food for pigs. " In scientific circles, however, Parmentier met with more understanding. Thanks to Lavoisier, the former army chemist was chosen to travel about France to investigate the reasons for the poor quality of bread. On his return, Parmentier drew up a long report on how to make bread from potatoes without mixing flour.

One day he invited some friends to a dinner composed of potatoes prepared in twenty different ways. Among the dozen guests were Benjamin Franklin, d'Alembert, Lavoisier, and a young Swedish diplomat whose love affairs were already causing much gossip: Axel de Fersen.

During the dinner, one of the guests exclaimed:

" But why don't you raise these potatoes yourself? "

Which is precisely what Parmentier was doing in the open country around Sablons, the field guarded by soldiers, the better to excite the curiosity of the people.

Parmentier died on December 17, 1813. Three years later, French pharmacists, both civilian and military, vied with one another to raise a monument over his tomb in the Père Lachaise cemetery in Paris; 38 th division, second row of graves, on the right of the avenue des Acacias.

Every year, in the month of August, potatoes bloom there.

LOUIS XVI THINKS ONLY OF EATING

Louis XVI did not inherit Louis XV's delicate taste in food. Like the Sun

King, he was a glutton and in addition, an ignoramus in culinary matters.

At the state banquet on his marriage night, as he stuffed himself until he almost choked, his grandfather warned:

" Come now! Don't overload your stomach! "

" Why not? " Louis replied, helping himself again and copiously: " I sleep much better when I've dined well. "

Later, during his trial, he interrupted the reading of the indictment to ask for a piece of bread. The moment he returned to the Temple after the verdict that condemned him to death, he sat down at the table and devoured " six cutlets, a large piece of chicken and some eggs; he drank two glasses of white wine and a glass of *Alicante* before falling asleep. "

During their reign Louis and Marie-Antoinette dined every Sunday in public. But the queen only pretended to eat: she disliked being stared at as if she were a strange animal and she didn't want people to see the movement of her jaws deforming her lovely face. She dined afterwards in her apartments, among her intimates.

All important courtiers were obliged to keep open house at least three times a week. Durfort de Cheverny writes in his Memoirs, about Choiseul:

" He dined precisely at two o'clock with all the foreigners who had been presented and the courtiers who had been received. The main table was laid for thirty-five persons and there was another table all ready. A footman counted the guests as they entered and as soon as the number exceeded thirty-five, the other table was laid. The vast quantity of silver tableware was magnificent, and lent a brilliant lustre. "

Bombe glacée triumphed. People had discovered that ices aided the digestion; they were served at the end of every important banquet.

At Strasbourg, Jean-Joseph Close, the pastry-cook-chef invented *pâté de foie gras with truffles* (1782); *foie gras* was already known, but Close discovered a way to strengthen and concentrate the prime ingredient. He perfected his discovery by surrounding it with a forcemeat of veal and chopped pork fat.

There was only one relatively discordant note: people continued to eat enormous amounts of garlic which was said to be a prophylactic... against the pest.

" Though our little mistresses dread it, " writes Bernardin de Saint-Pierre, " it is perhaps the most powerful remedy there is against the vapors and those nervous ills to which they are subject. "

THE FRENCH CUISINE IS ENRICHED BY BEEFSTEAK

Though we shall speak at length of Brillat-Savarin further on, it seems

opportune here to transcribe one of his reports on that fastidious era:

" *All the professions in which the aim is to prepare or to sell food, such as cooks, caterers,* pâtissiers, *confectioners, grocers, have multiplied on an ever increasing scale... Physics and chemistry have been called to the aid of cooking. The most distinguished intellects have not thought it beneath them to occupy themselves with our basic needs and have introduced improvements in it from the workingman's simple* pot-au-feu *to the transparent extracts which are served only in gold or crystal.*

" *Wines of all countries have been cultivated, imported and served according to protocol; Madeira which paves the way for the meal, the wines of France which are divided among the courses and those of Spain which crown the meal.*

" *The French cuisine has appropriated foreign dishes such as caviar and beef-steak; seasonings such as curry and soya... Coffee has become popular in the morning as nourishment and after dinner as an exhilarating and tonic drink.* "

This was the period when Beauvillier opened the first restaurant (1782) and created a profession " which commands a fortune every time the man who pursues it has good faith, orderliness and skill. "

The word " restaurant " does not come from Beauvillier but from a certain Boulanger, a vendor of soup on the rue Bailleul. The latter gave the name of " restaurant " to his soups, when he inscribed on his sign: " *Boulanger sells magical restoratives (restaurants).* " (1765).

It is Beauvillier in any case who first noticed that a foreigner or a traveler from the provinces could not dine suitably in Paris unless he were invited to the house of friends. Inns served meals to their boarders to be sure, but it was only " pot luck. "

Beauvillier was obliged to close his restaurant during the Revolution. But the idea was launched. When he resumed his activities, he was no longer alone. Others became *restaurateurs;* Robert, the brothers Véry, Meot, Rose, Legacque and especially Baleine whose *Rocher de Cancale*, on the rue Montorgueil, was rapidly to become the best in gastronomy.

The term " *coteaux* " is seldom used nowadays to designate lovers of good food who can tell the year and the source of a wine after the first sip. They are now called gastronomes.

The actor Desessarts (1738-1793) was among the best known in his day. Even today certain people claim that his way with aphorisms makes him the precursor of Brillat-Savarin.

His real name was Denis Dechanel. He was an attorney in Langres, his native town when, during a visit to Paris, one of his friends took him to the Comédie-Française. He emerged from that experience enthusiastic and determined... to become an actor.

Desessarts was a very large man. He had to have a genuine talent to

J.-B. Huet

Supper *(Photo Giraudon)*

make the public forget his obesity.
Moreover, he was also as great a gourmand as he was a gourmet. His
appetite was prodigious: he ate at one
meal enough to feed four ot five men.

" Though he was a gourmand, "
Émile Deschanel relates in his *Histoire
des Comédiens*, " he was also very
witty. A good dinner put him in fine
spirits. He analyzed the quality of
each dish eloquently and invented a
combination of words to describe it
that was amusingly whimsical.

" If the guests were agreeable and
hearty eaters, Desessarts' Pantagruelian gaiety reached lyrical heights and
expressed itself poetically... "

Desessarts' best friend was the actor
Dugazon, one of his colleagues in the
French theatre. Dugazon took upon
himself the joyful task of never losing
an opportunity to play a joke on his

colleague and to tease him about his
great girth.

One day when an elephant in the zoo
had just died, Dugazon told Desessarts
that the Minister of Sciences had
invited them to dinner along with a
certain number of their theatrical
colleagues.

" Good! Good! " cried Desessarts,
delighted at the thought of having an
excellent meal, " how shall I dress ? "

" In mourning, my dear fellow, in
deep mourning: the minister has just
lost someone dear to him and it would
be in the worst taste to appear in anything but black. "

Of course at the minister's reception—for there really was a luncheon in
honor of the French actors—only the
bigbellied Desessarts appeared in
deep mourning. And the incorrigible
Dugazon introduced him as follows:

BETWEEN TWO RICHES, ONE MUST CHOOSE *(Photo Josse Lalance)*

" Here, *Monsieur le Ministre*, is my good colleague, Desessarts. He is so moved by the cruel loss your zoological department has just sustained that he could not refrain from wearing mourning for the defunct pachyderm. "

Desessarts didn't find the joke funny. Two days later, Dugazon and Desessarts—followed by their witnesses—met on the duelling grounds. But as he was about to up his sword,

Dugazon looked at his enormous colleague and went up to him:

" My dear fellow, " he said, " I really hesitate to pit myself against you. You offer me such an enormous surface. I have too much advantage; let me make the game more equal! "

Dugazon then took out a piece of chalk and traced a circle on Desessarts' stomach.

" I want to be fair, " he added,

" any thrust sustained outside of this circle will not count. "

The adventure ended, it goes without saying, not with a death, but...with an excellent dinner in the course of which big, fat Desessarts uttered some of his best aphorisms:

" Good cooking is the food of a pure conscience. "

" A leg of lamb should be anticipated like the first meeting of lovers, mortified as a liar caught in the act, golden as a young German girl and bloody as a Carib. "

" Mutton is to lamb what a millionaire uncle is to his poverty-stricken nephew. "

" Never forget that the pheasant must be awaited like the pension of a man of letters who has never indulged in epistles to Ministers nor written madrigals for their mistresses. "

" Make the egg an amicable mediator who comes between different parts (of food) to bring about difficult reconciliations. "

RECIPES FOR COOKING " PARMENTIERS "(POTATOES)

POMMES DE TERRE FARCIES   STUFFED POTATOES

1. *Bake in a slow oven a dozen beautiful potatoes. When they are done, open them neatly on the side and scoop out the pulp with a little spoon, leaving only the skin which you set aside. 2. Rub the pulp through a sieve and mix with butter, fresh cream, the yolks of two eggs, some grated Gruyère cheese and salt. 3. Fill the skins of the potatoes with this mixture. Next, arrange them on a well-buttered pan. Heat in a slow oven for half an hour and serve (Richardin).*

POMMES DE TERRE A LA CHOISEUL   POTATOES A LA CHOISEUL

1. *Peel your potatoes and boil them in salted water. 2. Reduce them to a purée in a casserole, with a little butter and a spoonful of orange-flower water. Add a little salt and a good half glass of water. Heat for several minutes. 3. When your dough is smoothly blended and well thickened, add a little water to a couple of beaten eggs, add the eggs to the dough and make little balls which you toss into hot fat. Remove them carefully. Sprinkle with sugar when ready to serve (Recipe of the era).*

LUNCHEON AT MALMAISON *(Photo Josse Lalance)*

Eighth Course

NAPOLÉON
IS BETTER ON HORSEBACK
THAN AT THE TABLE

The French Revolution marks, in its first years, a certain slowing down in the " culinary " evolution of the country.

" At that time people had other things to think about than making clear broths and roasts, and writing up menus, " writes La Reynière. " The poor cooks were forgotten for a while: people reacted sternly against the extravagances of the past. It was considered good form to live like Spartans. "

But not for long. Soon the arts of the gourmet and the pleasures of the table reclaimed their prestige: the new leaders of France quickly tired of Spartan virtues. People began to eat well again, not only in Paris, but also in the provinces.

Cooks whose masters had emigrated were snapped up. Great houses reorganized. New restaurants were opened. The cuisine of France regained the grandeur it had enjoyed during the reign of Louis XV. It even became more refined.

However, what with wars and the gory horrors of the Terror, famine raged again for several years. In 1793 an ordinance prohibited more than one pound of meat a week per person— under pain of death! There was no bread and the potato crop was poor.

95

But restrictions are never applied to all—under any regime. And while plain people, guilty of having yielded to the temptation of the table, were rushed to the guillotine, there were feasting and carousing in the mansions of Barras and Fouché (1).

The following is the menu of a dinner served by Barras in the winter of 1793:

SOUP

With little onions, *à la ci-devant minime*

SECOND COURSE

Steaks of sturgeon *en brochette*

SIX ENTRÉES

Turbot sauté *à l'homme de confiance*, formerly Maître-d'hôtel
Eel à la Tartare
Cucumber stuffed with marrow
Vol au vent of chicken breasts with Béchamel sauce
A *ci-devant* Saint-Pierre sauce with capers
Fillets of partridge in rings (not to say in a crown)

TWO ROASTS

Gudgeons of the region
A carp in court-bouillon

FIFTH COURSE (entremets)

Lentils *à la ci-devant Reine*

---

(1) Right in the midst of famine, but also in a revolutionary atmosphere.

96

Beets scalded and sautéd in butter
Artichoke bottoms *à la ravigote*
Eggs *à la neige*
Cream fritters with orange water

SALAD

Celery *en rémoulade*

DESSERT

Twenty-four different dishes

This menu is annotated by Barras himself. He notes that it contains too much fish: " Take out the gudgeons, " he orders. And finally he cautions his servants not to forget to place cushions on the chairs of mesdames Tallien, Talma, Beauharnais, Hingerelot and Osbirande...

ALL PARISIANS AT THE SAME TABLE

This, in short, was the era of communal meals. They were launched the year after the Fall of the Bastille by Monsieur de Saint-Ange, a " progressive " aristocrat, who was eager to play his part in the new Regime. He convinced the citizens of Paris that they owed it to themselves to celebrate each year the glorious anniversary of the 14th of July... by keeping open house in front of their mansions.

" Thus, " he declared, " Paris will become one huge family: more than a million people will sit down together at the same table. Toasts will be drunk to the ringing of all the bells, the booming of guns, the salvos of musketry... at the same moment and in every quarter of the city at the same time. "

Those communal suppers lasted but a short time: they did not produce the excellent results expected.

SOUPLESS SUPPERS EXCEPT IN MÉAS

The Revolution was not merely political: it also changed many customs of the French people. The four meals (breakfast, lunch, dinner and supper) were reduced to two: breakfast and dinner. The latter was soon the more important of the two.

The Russian nobleman Karamzine who traveled through part of France after the Terror wrote:

" Everywhere, even in the poorest villages, we find good inns, an ample supply of food and clean bedrooms with a fireplace. For a dinner for two we pay three *livres* and ten *sous*, which is not dear. "

Karamzine notes with astonishment that in certain inns, soup is no longer served: " We sup without soup, " and also that the traveler finds only spoons and forks on the table: everyone brings his own knife.

At Méas, in the Pyrenees, another traveler, Monsieur de Saint-Amans, was surprised by a different soup story.

" To make soup, " he writes, " the peasant woman takes her pot and goes to draw water from the mountain stream; for they have never seen such an object as a pitcher at Méas... The pot is brought back and hung over a fire of junipers, the only wood used here for heating. While waiting for the water to heat, she prepares bread in a large wooden dish with a little lump of butter... At last the water boils: she pours it boiling hot (on the bread), adds a clove of garlic and a raw onion, which the cook chews to a mash and spits out into the soup (sic). "

Intrigued—anyone would be— Monsieur de Saint-Amans inquired what name was given to this recipe. " Humph! Soup à Méas, " was the answer.

An Englishman by the name of Young, who was also traveling in France at that period, complained of being exploited:

" At Nemours, an innkeeper outdid all the others in France in knavish tricks. For dinner we had: a thin soup, a partridge and a roast chicken, a dish of celery, a little cauliflower and two bottles of local wine. And for dessert, only two biscuits and four apples.

" That rascal dared to present us with the following extravagant bill: soup, one *livre* and ten *sous*; wine, two livres and four *sous*; partridge, two *livres* and ten *sous*; chicken, two *livres*; celery, one *livre* and four *sous*; cauliflower, two *livres*; bread and dessert, two *livres*.

" When I tried to tell him what I thought of him, he had already fled behind his ovens, the ruffian. "

" At Meaux, " another traveler declares, " they have good meat and good bread. And also fairly good fruit... but the wine of Brie is utterly worthless. "

THE " NAPOLÉON OF PRESERVED FOOD " IS ALSO BETRAYED BY THE ENGLISH

The eighteenth century was drawing to a close.

In Paris, in a shabby little atelier on the rue de la Folie-Méricourt a greying quadragenarian was about to make the year 1795 one of the greatest dates in the history of the French cuisine. His name: François Appert. Little is known about him: the Napoléon of preserved food did not have a Las Cases. He was born around 1750, perhaps in Massuy, in the Seine-et-Oise, or else at Chalon-sur-Saône, or Châlons-sur-Marne. All three towns claim him as their native son.

At first a salesman of champagne, François Appert became a confectioner on the rue des Lombards, before he settled down in sordid quarters on the rue de la Folie-Méricourt. There he conceived the idea of destroying the fermentation that caused animal and vegetable substances to spoil, by subjecting them to extremely high heat. In 1795, he enclosed some food in hermetically sealed wide-mouthed bottles and boiled them in a *bain-marie*.

Before Appert, many seekers had tried to improve the techniques for preserving food. Drying, smoking and salting were the most widely used methods. They were not satisfactory: the food treated by these methods caused scurvy.

At the beginning of the wars of the Empire, the provisions for the troops caused the Emperor much anxiety. Chaptal called Napoléon's attention to Appert's invention, and as a result, Appert was appointed official purveyor to the Grande Armée—both to his delight and his misfortune! He set up a factory at Massy in which as many as fifty employees worked. However, several specimens of glass bottles in which meat, fish and vegetables could be preserved for three months fell into the hands of English technicians.

The English promptly realized the profit they could derive from the Frenchman's discovery, especially if they could substitute metal for glass. They were successful: and in 1814, the first tins were put out by the Donkin-Hall factories. The British did not hesitate to assume credit for the invention and to take out patents on it. The Americans followed suit, but had the decency to pay public tribute to the French inventor before they raised preserving to the status of a national industry.

What became of Appert?

In 1809 the Emperor granted him a reward of twelve thousands *livres* and, three years later, the title of Benefactor of Humanity... Which did not prevent the Napoléon of preserves from dying in sordid poverty and almost starving to death. The man who had given the world the means to store provisions had never made any for himself.

ALL THE SECRETS OF " CHICKEN A LA MARENGO "

Chicken à la Marengo was born on June 14, 1800, during the Italian campaign. It was two o'clock in the afternoon: the French had lost two battles since eight o'clock that morning. Desaix—who was to die that evening—suggested engaging in a third: in the distance, Austrian dispatch-riders were dashing towards Vienna to announce their victory.

" Do what you please, " Bonaparte told Desaix. " As for me, I am going to eat. " He motioned to his steward.

" I fear, " said the latter, " that the meal will not meet with your approval. Those cursed Austrians have intercepted our canteens: there is no butter in the kitchens. "

The First Consul made a vague gesture and sat down at the table. An hour later General Desaix was again on the road to victory and " chicken à la Marengo " sautéd in oil had become history.

At Lunéville, a year later, at the time of the signing of the treaty with Austria Cambacérès complained to Bonaparte because he had delayed the arrival of a courier delivering boxes of perishable supplies and the finest foods. The First Consul tapped him on the shoulder. " Console yourself, my poor Cambacérès. In future those couriers will arrive on time and will continue to bring your turkeys, your truffles, your Strasbourg pâtés, your hams from Mainz. "

" I thank you for that, Your Excellency... How do you expect us to make friends if we can't give them choice food? You know yourself that men are ruled largely by what they eat. "

NAPOLÉON'S REPAST AT THE TUILERIES
(Photo Bulloz)

Bonaparte nodded, although he himself was seldom to use that policy. He preferred to leave it to Cambacérès, to Talleyrand, to some of his best generals.

Even in the sumptuous days of the Empire, Napoléon never conformed with good grace to the ceremonies of the table. He ate quickly and gluttonously. After the meal, Constant, his valet, sometimes had to bring him clean garments to replace those he had spotted. At any hour of the day or night, his meals had to be ready to be served on call. His breakfasts, which he was apt to take from six o'clock in the morning on, were most often served to him on a little mahogany pedestal table, incrusted with mother-of-pearl: eggs fried in butter, a salad of beans and, for dessert, some Parmesan cheese or two olives.

Dinner was a heartier meal. The Emperor ate between six o'clock in the evening and two, three or even four o'clock in the morning, depending on his work or his audiences.

He liked to eat alone. He was served a great number of dishes, each one under a cover which the Emperor lifted himself. He would keep the dishes he liked and return the others to the kitchen.

" How is it I never eat pork *crépinettes* (small, flat sausages)? " he asked Danau, his maître d'hôtel, one day testily.

" Sire, that is not a choice dish. "

" I don't care! I want some *crépinettes*. "

The next day Danau had crépinettes of pheasant prepared for his master. Napoléon clapped his hands (sic) and helped himself three times. A month later, the maître d'hôtel gave it to him again.

" What's this! " cried Napoléon in angry disgust, " I'll have none of these hostler's dishes! "

The Emperor would not allow string beans to be served. He was afraid of finding strings in them which, he said, felt like hairs in his mouth.

At the siege of Cherbourg, when he was inspecting quarters and walked past the camp kitchen, he asked for a plate of " ration soup. " It was served to him. He grimaced in disgust: there was a hair in the plate! Napoléon looked around, saw his old guard watching him, petrified with respect. The Emperor calmly went on eating his soup—he even asked for a second helping!

" The most extraordinary thing, " Constant relates, " is that there was also a hair in the second plate. "

LAGUIPIÈRE, HEAD COOK IN THE IMPERIAL KITCHENS

Napoléon was fond of starches, potatoes, beans, lentils and especially of pastas *à l'italienne* of which he consumed a full plate at least once a day. He never ate bread.

Among cooked dishes—if one can believe Constant his faithful valet—his preferences leaned to *Boudin à la Richelieu* (blood pudding served on stewed apples fragrant with cinnamon), ragoût of mutton, *quenelles* (force-meat balls). For dessert, nothing pleased him so much as macaroni timbales *à la Milanaise*.

His favorite wine was a Chambertin, diluted with water. He never drank alcohol or liqueur but ended every meal with a cup of coffee.

Being employed as a chef at the Imperial court was no sinecure. The kitchens were poorly ventilated; wages never exceeded 2,400 francs. In fact Napoléon had the reputation of paying his personel poorly. In one of his books, Frédéric Masson gives us the list of the master-cooks who followed one another at the Imperial ranges:

"First Gaillon, who had accompanied the general to Egypt and who was retired with the position of *Garde de Bouche* to Fontainebleau; then Danger who also made the campaign in Egypt and had even been in danger of death when, on the return journey, the silverware was stolen six leagues from Aix-en-Provence. Followed by, one after the other, from 1802: Venard de la Borde, Coulon, Farcy, Laguipière, Debray, Leconte, Heurtin, Lemoigne. Ferdinand was the cook on the Island of Elba; a certain Dousseau, head-cook during the Hundred Days. And finally Chandelier at St-Helena. "

Of them all only one became famous: Laguipière. We see him for the first time in the kitchens of the Comte d'Estaing, when the latter disembarked on the Island of Granada in 1775. Antonin Carême acknowledged Laguipière as his master and declared that he was one of the greatest masters of French cooking.

After leaving the Imperial kitchens, Laguipière entered the service of Murat whom he accompanied to Naples and then to the Russian campaigns. He froze to death in Vilna during the retreat of 1812. Unfortunately he left none of his recipes to posterity.

A PERFECT GENTLEMAN: THE MARQUIS LOUIS DE CUSSY

We cannot leave Napoléon without mentioning a gentleman of quality who was also a discriminating gastronome: the Marquis de Cussy (1), Prefect of the Palais and chief steward in the Emperor's household, author of

_____
(1) Louis de Cussy (1767-1841).

" *L'Art Culinaire* " which, unfortunately, is practically impossible to find today.

Of Cussy, Alexandre Dumas père said:

" He was one of those apostles who have all the necessary qualities for making converts: he felt an affectionate and deeply respectful gratitude that amounted almost to a religion for the benefits he had received from Marie-Antoinette as well as for the affection Napoléon showed him. "

Cussy had squandered an immense fortune and so was reduced to working.

Napoléon was very fond of him. " He is my wet-nurse!... " he said of him.

Nothing could be bought for the Emperor until Cussy had given his approval. He watched over everything; clothes, furniture to be replaced, food to be supplied for the Court. Evil tongues even declared that M. de Cussy would not tolerate having a young beauty admitted by night to the Emperor's apartments, until, as a good servant, he had studied her " from all aspects " (sic). He himself claimed that he had saved his master from the " Naples sickness " on several occasions.

Cussy received once a week.

" Isn't tomorrow the day for your coquettes, Cussy ? " the Emperor, who delighted in teasing him, would often ask.

" No, Sire... only my coquetry! "

On the eve of Napoléon's departure for Elba, Cussy was ordered to accompany Marie-Louise to Vienna. He accepted the mission, but the Empress appeared to be so little affected by the separation that soon, sick at heart, the Chief Steward returned to France. He arrived in Paris one day before the Emperor: it was Cussy who welcomed Napoléon at the Tuileries.

After the Hundred Days and Waterloo, Louis XVIII refused at first to interest himself in the fate of the Emperor's faithful servant. But when he learned that Cussy was the " inventor " of *fraises à la Cussy* (strawberries à la Cussy)—strawberries, cream and champagne—he gave him back his old position.

The Chief Steward's last years were darkened by a cruel illness—cancer—which he bore with admirable patience. Physicians experimented on him with new remedies, but they only hastened his death (1841).

A FEW RECIPES *A LA* APPERT

ASPERGES EN BOUTEILLE   *CANNED ASPARAGUS*

Cut up asparagus in a length suitable for standing them upright in a wide-mouthed jar. Or place them head down, and, with a little stick arrange them so that their axis is parallel to that of the receptacle.

When several jars have been filled, put them, uncovered, in a boiler which must come up to two-thirds of their height ; then quickly cover. The caps must have an opening to allow the water to spout out after the air in the jar has been expelled by pressure on the cap. After that you close the opening tightly and seal it.

HARICOTS VERTS EN BOUTEILLE   *CANNED STRING BEANS*

String the beans and put them in a large earthenware pot ; pour over them some boiling water and leave them in this water for several minutes ; then take them out and let them drain. The beans are then tossed into lightly salted boiling water until they are almost cooked ; they should however be a little crisp ; strain them and sauté them in butter with a little parsley. Let them cool, put them with their sauce in the jar and boil in a bain-marie not more than five minutes.

For green flageolets en bouteille, proceed as above. But boil in a bain-marie for three minutes only.

TOMATES EN BOUTEILLE   *TOMATOES EN BOUTEILLE*

Choose very ripe and very firm tomatoes. Cut them in pieces if they are too large ; put them in a pan containing some cold water and heat them slowly. As they rise to the surface, take them out with a skimming ladle and put them in cold water to firm them. That done, place them in the jars with a solution of about 4 tablespoons of salt for every quart of water and place them in a bain-marie for a quarter of an hour, or in the pressure cooker ten minutes.

POULET MARENGO   *CHICKEN A LA MARENGO* (historic recipe)

1. Cut up a chicken in pieces and brown in oil, putting in first the legs and thighs which take longer to cook. Salt, pepper, add a few spices, and a bouquet garni and a handful of mushrooms.

2. While the chicken cooks gently, prepare in another casserole a roux moistened with a cup of consommé to which you add a glass of Madeira and a glass of white wine. Stir and add little by little some oil in which the chicken has fricasséed. Add the sautéed chicken to the sauce with a handful of mushrooms. Continue cooking till meat is very tender.

BASKETS FOR CENTERPIECES, EMPIRE STYLE *(Photo Josse Lalance)*

Ninth Course

CAMBACÉRÈS
AND GRIMOD
DE LA REYNIÈRE

If Napoléon was not a gastronome, he nevertheless occupies an important place in the history of French cooking through a third person.

" Entertain in my place, " he ordered the Arch-Chancellor Cambacérès, " and let your table do honor to France. "

" Entertain, " he said to Talleyrand his minister. " Give a dinner for thirty-six people four times a week. See that all men of importance in France and all foreign friends are invited. "

Both Cambacérès and Talleyrand were ideally suited to play the part of an Amphitryon.

A man of average height, with black eyes and an intelligent and expressive face, Cambacérès was a conscientious though slightly capricious gourmand. Antonin Carême has written that the Arch-Chancellor's table did not deserve its great reputation—testimony which is unreliable: Carême's viperish pen spat scorn on all those who did not shower him with gold or who did not consider him the center of the universe. Even his praise of certain of his colleagues is tinged with jealousy.

At Cambacérès' the great dinners—always about fifty guests—were held twice a week, Tuesdays and Saturdays, the dinner on Saturday being the more elaborate. In four courses, sixteen to eighteen different dishes were served.

NO GUEST IS LATE AT THE ARCH-CHANCELLOR'S DINNERS

No one was allowed to arrive late at the Arch-Chancellor's. The dinners began at 5:30 under the Consulate, at 6 o'clock under the Empire. Never did the master of the house delay, even for a minute, the time for sitting down at table.

The first time he was invited, Prince William of Bavaria was obliged to go away without being admitted to the dining-room where all the guests were already seated. The prince did not even have a chance to plead that he was in Paris for the first time in his life and that his coachman had been caught in a traffic jam.

Dinner was served in a vast dining-room, lighted by a great round lamp of richly chiseled gilded bronze. On the long table, covered with a cloth of Brussels lace, ten three-branched candelabra cast a thousand twinkling lights. As soon as the guests were seated, the doors leading to the three salons were shut. During the meal, which lasted two hours at least, the salons were crowded with a throng of other guests, who were not invited to dinner, but simply to greet the Arch-Chancellor. For them cold buffet was provided.

Cambacérès ate with complete absorption. When the conversation around him became too loud, he would cry out: " Don't talk so loud, I beg you. A man can't know what he is eating. "

HOW THE ARCH-CHANCELLOR ISSUED HIS INVITATIONS

The Arch-Chancellor, a bachelor, was very fond of women (his affairs set tongues wagging). And yet he never invited more than a small and select number of them to his dinners. Moreover he insisted that the ladies should appear in lavish gowns and adorn themselves with sumptuous jewels. To the Duchesse de La Rochefoucauld, who was not dressed elaborately enough to suit his taste, he remarked one evening:

" That's a very charming négligé you have there, Madame ! "

" Monseigneur, " replied the Duchesse who was quick at repartee, " I beg you to excuse me... I have just come from the Empress' and I did not have time to change. "

When the dinner was over, the master of the house rose while, at a sign from him, lackeys wearing liveries of red and black velvet with guilloche buttons flung open the doors of the salons where the courtiers and petitioners waited. With a majestic step, Cambacérès passed among the groups, chatting with some, ignoring others. From time to time the Arch-Chancellor would beckon to his secretary, always a few steps behind him, and speak to him in a low tone. The secretary would then go up to the person his master had just left and announce in ringing tones: " His Serene Highness invites you to dine on Tuesday. "

THE ILLUSTRIOUS CARÊME AND HIS SLANDERS

Bitter though his comments were we must nevertheless report the comments of Antonin Carême on those dinners of the Arch-Chancellor:

" Cambacérès took a meticulous interest in every detail concerning his table, " he writes, " but only to quarrel about it and to cut down expenses. In him one noticed in the highest degree that care and that anxiety about details so indicative of the miser.

" At each course he noted the entrées that had not been touched or which were barely eaten: and the next day

CAMBACÉRÈS *(Photo Josse Lalance)*

he made up the menu with those vile leftovers.

" What a dinner! Good heavens!... I do not mean to say that the leftovers should not be served: I mean that it is not a dinner fit for a prince and an eminent gastronome. This is a very delicate point: the master should say nothing, see nothing: the probity and skill of the cook must be the deciding factors. The leftovers must be served with precaution, skill and especially in silence.

" The Arch-Chancellor received from various departments innumerable presents of articles of food and the most beautiful fowl. All that was hidden away in a huge pantry to which only the prince had the key. He kept a record of the provisions and of the date of arrival and he himself gave the order to use them: food never appeared on his table until after it had lost its freshness.

" Cambacérès was never a gourmand in the accepted sense of the word; but he was a tremendous and even voracious eater. Could one believe that he would prefer above all dishes *paté chaud aux boulettes* (hot patties with meat balls), a dull, heavy dish! What parsimony! What a pity! What a house! "

If Cambacérès took a personal interest in his household, it was because he did not want to be fleeced by his servants or be taken in by his master-cook!... As we have said it is better to mistrust the slanders of that illus-trious Carême (as he called himself, with characteristic modesty). Aside from Tuesdays and Saturdays, the doors of the Hôtel d'Elbeuf, near the Carrousel—and later, that of the rue Saint-Florentin—were open only to the Arch-Chancellor's intimate friends.

The two most assiduous guests were the little, fat rolypoly d'Aigrefeuille and the long, gaunt Villevielle. With Cambacérès they formed a trio of gourmets as famous as they were inseparable. Later, when the Restoration turned against the Arch-Chancellor, Aigrefeuille and Villevielle were the only faithful companions he had left. All the others, the family friends, the flatterers, the petitioners of happier days, turned their backs while the populace sang:

" As d'Aigrefeuille can no longer sponge on Monseigneur, he has draped his fork in crêpe to show his grief. " And about Cambacérès himself:

" The Duc de Parme no longer keeps open house for courtiers, Monseigneur eats cheese but it's no longer Parmesan. "

It was to d'Aigrefeuille (1745-1818) that Grimod de la Reynière dedicated his first *Almanach des Gourmets ;*

" To the charming man who possesses the art, so difficult and so uncommon, of getting the best out of an excellent repast. "

Grimod did not dare to dedicate it to Cambacérès himself. Later on, however, the Arch-Chancellor gladly accepted an invitation to preside over the famous " *Jury-dégustateur* " (Jury of Tasters) created by Grimod de la Reynière " to pass judgment on the quality of foodstuffs and their skilful preparation. "

If the chair was vacant it was because the first President of the society, Dr Joseph Gastaldi, had just died a glorious death, not on the battlefield of Austerlitz, but struck down by an attack of apoplexy on the evening of December 2, 1805, at the table of Mgr du Belloy, the Archbishop of Paris. He was about to help himself for the fourth time to salmon.

Every month, therefore, around the well-filled table of the " *Jury-dégustateur,* " Cambacérès met his inseparables, Villevielle and d'Aigrefeuille, and also, among other members of that honorable assembly, the amiable President of the Supreme Court of Appeals, Henrion de Pansey who did not hesitate to say:

" I consider the discovery of a new dish which excites our appetite and prolongs our enjoyment as a much more interesting event than the discovery of a star, for we always know enough about that. And I shall not consider the sciences as sufficiently honored until I see a chef seated in the Institute. "

There too, Cambacérès saw General Bisson (1787-1811), a former soldier's son, a man capable of challenging his host for a poor dinner! His innumerable wounds—and his obesity— prevented him from engaging in the last struggles of the Empire. He was to die in his bed at Mantua. His name is on the *Arc de Triomphe*. Of him, Napoléon said:

" I always have triple rations allotted to him in the field. He is a fine, an excellent officer. On the battlefield he is a Goliath; but in the city he is a veritable Gargantua who has to have a beef a day as an appetizer! "

The *Jury-dégustateur* sometimes invited actresses, pretty women to their reunions. They called them their " culinary sisters. " Of course, those charming guests were not permitted to participate in their deliberations.

And then, there was Grimod de la Reynière, Grimod the magnificent!

THE MOST FANTASTIC HOST OF ALL

To relate all the adventures, the pranks of this personage worthy of the pen of a Molière, is impossible... It would take a whole volume. Grimod de la Reynière's family came from Lyon. His grandfather died there on the field of honor... like Gastaldi: but with him it was *foie gras* that killed him. His father, a farmer general, made a fortune in pigs. His mother, of very noble origins, was a stickler for etiquette.

Grimod had no hands. He lost them, he claimed, in a " family accident. " When he was only a few weeks old, a sow was said to have come up to his cradle and eaten his hands.

He used his stumps with remarkable skill: some people said they looked like the claws of a lobster, others like duck's webs. Balthasar—his Christian name—was born in Paris in 1758 in the splendid private mansion his father had built on the corner of the rue des Champs Elysées and the Place Louis XV. There—and later in his château of Villiers-sur-Orge—our hero was to give the best examples of his genius for macabre humor.

His law studies finished, he became a member of the bar. His first day, to attract attention, he stationed a giant and a dwarf disguised as musketeers at the door of the de la Reynière mansion. When a visitor appeared, the two musketeers rushed forward and enquired:

" Whom do you wish to see? Monsieur de la Reynière the father, the exploiter of the people, or Monsieur de la Reynière the son, defender of widows and orphans? "

Another time, he took advantage of his parents' absence from Paris to send dinner invitations to his father's friends and tradesmen, as well as to his mother's relatives. As servants to wait on the dinner guests he corralled

GRIMOD DE LA REYNIÈRE
(Photo Josse Lalance)

112

from the place de Grève some beggars whom he masqueraded as heralds-at-arms from the Middle-Ages. Children, swinging censers (1), stood at the entrance to the salons. The guests were amazed.

" That is to keep you from glorifying the masters of the house as you have formed a habit of doing, " retorted Grimod.

The abashed guests had not come to the end of their surprises. As they entered the dining room, they raised their heads: up above the door, the *enfant terrible* had written the following four commandments:

Don't put a dirty knife or spoon on the tablecloth.

Don't sound like a trumpet when you blow your nose at table.

Don't wipe your knife or fork on the tablecloth.

Don't look at your handkerchief after you have used it.

The guests entered and discovered, seated in the place of honor, an enormous live pig, clad in the magnificent apparel of Monsieur de la Reynière the elder. On the menu: nothing but pork.

" One of my relatives still in his natural state supplies me with all these meats! " Balthasar explained.

In the end the guests were enchanted and they decided to laugh at the adventure.

---

(1) Play on the word " encens ". Encenser means to swing the censer or to glorify.

But just when the dinner was at its height, Monsieur and Madame de la Reynière arrived unexpectedly. This time Balthasar had gone too far! The next day an order under the King's private seal—the father had connections in high places—exiled Balthasar Grimod de la Reynière, in disgrace, to the Canon of Domeure, near Nancy. He had been there only two years when his father died leaving him—to his regret—an immense fortune.

HOW TO JUDGE ONE'S REAL FRIENDS

From that moment Grimod's eccentricity knew no bounds. With much noise and bluster he announced that he intended to invite all the lawyers in Paris to a gigantic dinner. He set a date. On the appointed day the guests arrived, delighted at the prospect of a magnificent feast. This time, former convicts in prison uniforms—dragging, instead of a ball and chain, Dutch cheeses painted black—were ordered to mingle among the guests. They allowed only those lawyers to enter who could show proof that they were commoners or that they had never condemned a client to prison.

Another time Grimod decided to test the friendship of the guests he was accustomed to entertaining. He locked the doors of his town-house and disappeared for two weeks. At the end of that time, his friends received an announcement of their host's death informing them that the obsequies would be held that same evening at five o'clock.

Few indeed were the friends who met in front of the mortuary door at the hour indicated. Nevertheless all the members of the *Jury-dégustateur* and all the " culinary sisters " were present, grouped behind their president the Arch-Chancellor Cambacérès.

The doors opened. The cortège was admitted into the salons whose walls had been draped in black. In the middle of one room: a coffin... from which Grimod soon emerged. Naturally the farce ended with an enormous dinner!

But the matter did not end there. A few days later, all the " absent friends " were invited in their turn. They were led into the dining room which was still draped in black. Around the table, chairs were replaced by coffins and the cover of each coffin bore the name of each one of the guests.

All those macabre pleasantries did not prevent Grimod from being a genuine gastronome. With real passion he contributed to perfecting the art of Good Eating and of Gastro-nomy. His *Manuel de l'Amphitryon* and his *Almanach des Gourmands* attest to this.

The illustrious Carême was never to forgive him. He refused to admit that anyone other than himself should take the liberty of writing a single line about cooking.

Grimod's other enemy was Monsieur de Talleyrand. Their misunderstanding dated back to the days of their youth: a woman had set them against each other. Grimod had outrivalled him with a pretty trollop: the future Bishop of Autun was never to forgive him for that victory.

When Dr. Gastaldi died, Talleyrand was certain that the honor of replacing him in the Presidency of the *Jury-dégustateur* could fall only to himself. He was mistaken. Grimod, friend of Cambacérès and founder of the assembly, had no difficulty in getting the Arch-Chancellor elected.

Talleyrand took a base revenge. He denounced Grimod to Fouché. The Prefect of Police summoned La Reynière and accused him of having openly made remarks unfavorable to Napoléon.

Grimod protested. Fouché then asked him:

" Come, come, monsieur! Between us, what do you think of the Emperor? "

" I think, " replied Balthasar, " that if Napoléon turned his genius to cooking, humanity would be all the happier. "

THE CONTENTED GASTRONOME *(Photo Josse Lalance)*

THERE IS NOTHING (AT A DINNER) LIKE THOSE LADIES OF THE THÉÂTRE FRANÇAIS

HE DIED IN THE CHATEAU DE LA BRINVILLIERS

Each month Grimod attended personally to the preparation of the dinner given by the *Jury-dégustateur*. Those dinners were held either at the house of one of the members, or of a " private individual " desirous of proving the excellence of his cuisine, or even in a select restaurant.

The rule required that a secret ballot be taken after each dish. Food and victuals were supplied gratis by merchants or wholesale dealers eager to obtain the famous certificate of " official recognition. " Such was the renown of the association that those who obtained the certificate—which Grimod and his group awarded very charily—immediately saw their clientèle doubled.

The " culinary sisters " were for the most part artists from the leading Parisian theaters: several of them were even from the Comédie-Française. Grimod explained this choice in his *Almanach des Gourmands*.

" We beg the pardon of all good women (or those whom the world has agreed to designate as such) but, as regards amiability, a seemly freedom and agreeable playfulness, we know no one at a dinner who can compare with most of the actresses from the French theatre. "

It was, of course, an actress from the Comédie-Française, Adélaïde-Thérèse Feuchère, whom the famous host married late in life. With her, in the twilight of his life, Grimod de la Reynière left his mansion on the Champs-Elysées for the ancient château de la Brinvilliers at Villiers-sur-Orge. There, the facetious Grimod was to give a last " display of fireworks. "

In the principal rooms of the château, secret doors were set in the wainscoting and traps were laid beneath the floors. Beds rested on a wheel which set in motion a screw and trestle. The next morning, thanks to this system, the guest would find himself ingeniously settled in a different room from the one in which he had gone to sleep. The result was a regular procession—each man hunting for his own clothes.

The memory of the celebrated poisoner (1) did not spoil Grimod's appetite. Alexandre Dumas père, invited by the famous gastronome, declares:

" He gave us the best dinner I have ever eaten. "

---

(1) Marie Madeleine d'Aubray, marquise de Brinvilliers, was beheaded and burned in Paris after one of the must famous trials of the XVIII th century.

That perfect lord of the table came to a worthy end—an end we could wish for all of us. Towards the end of a noteworthy dinner which he shared with only a few faithful friends, he dozed off. He never woke up again.

It was a midnight supper on Christmas Eve, December, 1837.

Grimod would soon have been eighty years old.

SOME OF
DE LA REYNIÈRE'S
EPICUREAN RULES

For a rich man the finest role in the world is that of host.

A gastronome-host who did not know how to carve or serve would be like the owner of a fine library who did not know how to read.

A good dinner being one of the greatest joys of man's life, let us love and honor him who gives it by going out of our way to eat him out of house and home. Let us pay our reckoning in merry remarks, pleasant sallies, erotic couplets, witty talk, amusing and short tales—short above all.

A real gourmand is never late.

Standing on ceremony when one is at the table always works to the detriment of the dinner. The great point is to eat hot, nicely and a great deal.

True gourmands have always finished their dinner before dessert. What they eat beyond the dessert is merely politeness; but in general they are very polite.

Women, who everywhere else are the charm of society, are out of place at a dinner of gourmands.

There is too much wine in the world for celebrating mass, but not enough to keep mill wheels turning. Therefore we must drink it.

The number thirteen is dangerous at the dinner table only when there is just enough to eat for twelve.

TALLEYRAND *(Photo Josse Lalance)*

Tenth Course

TALLEYRAND AND BRILLAT-SAVARIN

" The only master Talleyrand did not betray is the cheese of Brie, " one of the enemies of the Prince of Benevento remarked one day.

The ex-Bishop of Autun was one of the most lavish hosts of his day. Moreover his house found favor with that severe critic, Antonin Carême.

" Ah! what a difference between the ugly household of Monsieur de Cambacérès, " exclaims the latter, " and the great, noble dwelling of the Prince of Benevento... There only the freshest and finest products are used. There everything is skill, order, splendor; there talent is favored and held in honor. The chef rules the stomach. Who knows, perhaps he influences the Minister's thought: whether charming, keen or noble? "

Talleyrand noticed Antonin Carême for the first time just as the latter was ending his apprenticeship with the famous *pâtissier* Bailly, rue Vivienne. Did Carême eventually owe his career to Talleyrand? It is probable. The Minister of Foreign Affairs had an opportunity to recommend Marc-Antoine—Carême's real first name—to monarchs whose policy and secrets were highly important to France. From that to supposing that Carême supplied him with information is only a step.

ALL THE CLERGY
OF AUTUN ARE GUILTY
OF GOURMANDISE

Talleyrand spent one hour every morning in his kitchens. There he was completely free. He chatted with everyone on the staff, teased the servant girls. He questioned the lackeys as to what they had heard the guests say at dinner the night before. He also took a hand in planning the dinner for that evening.

His knowledge of culinary matters was excellent. He knew how to choose, according to the seasons of the year, among the many succulent dishes worthy to appear on his table. He knew how to draw a subtle distinction between the enormous number of pâtés among his reserve stores: goose-liver from Strasbourg, duck-liver from Toulouse, potted meats from Nérac, Bologna sausages from Lyon, cold sausages from Arles, tongues from Troyes.

At dinner, which for him was the principal meal of the day, Monsieur de Talleyrand preferred heavy dishes and light women. In the morning, several cups of camomile tea put him in shape for his work which he interrupted towards noon only to consume one or two soups.

Like every respectable host, Talleyrand reserved to himself the right to carve the poultry and meats at the table—an act he performed with much solemnity. He served his guests himself. Naturally the deference he showed lessened in the measure that the quality of his guests diminished.

" Will Your Highness do me the honor to accept this piece of beef? " he would murmur respectfully, as he filled the plate of a foreign monarch.

" Will Monseigneur take a little of this beef? " he would say, smiling at an important prelate.

The guests at the end of the table had to be satisfied with:

" Eh you! down there!... Who wants some beef?... beef!... beef! "

When, thanks to his father's connections, Talleyrand succeeded in getting himself appointed Bishop of Autun, he was already thinking of smoothing the way to the next legislative elections. He well knew that there is more success in casseroles than in legal records. Guests followed one after the other at his table: not the least zealous among them being members of the clergy... In the end, the high ecclesiastical authorities became alarmed. They threatened to excommunicate our bishop if he continued to encourage sins in general and gourmandise in particular.

The warning was sharp. Talleyrand decided to return to Paris and plead his own cause. On his arrival there, as he had a free evening, he wrote to Narbonne-Lira, his lifelong friend:

" You've heard the news! Come and dine with me and console me. Every-

one is going to turn me down completely. So this evening we'll just have
jellied meats and some wine on ice. "

TALLEYRAND
" HUNTER OF BEAVERS "

However, a Pantagruelian meal,
washed down with plenty of liquor,
almost robbed France forever of her
finest diplomat and the Art of Good
Eating of a marvelous epicurean.

A few years before, the young Abbé,
Charles-Maurice de Talleyrand-Périgord, had been sent to America—
through the mediation of Gouverneur
Morris—to help him forget his stormy
liaison with Madame de Flahaut.

While visiting Niagara Falls, the
young Frenchman was seized with such
" nausea " at the sight of " so much
water " that he, with the two friends
accompanying him, decided to take a
stimulant on the spot. No sooner said
than done: on corn whiskey they lost
consciousness to the point of... signing
up with a gang of beaver trappers.
Useless to describe the stupor and
dismay of the future Bishop of Autun
when he came to his senses. The affair
was settled *in extremis*.

That youthful adventure was the
source of Talleyrand-Périgord's mis-
trust of alcohol. Though he ate a great
deal, he drank little—which did not
prevent him from describing the art
of sampling fine champagne:

" You take your glass in the hollow
of your hand, you warm it, you twirl
it around in a circular motion so that
the alcohol gives off its perfume. Next,
you raise it to your nostrils, inhale it
and then you put down your glass and
'talk about it.' "

TALLEYRAND
AND THE SALMON

Madame de Flahaut—Talleyrand's
one-time mistress—(they had a son,
Charles de Flahaut, father of the Duc
de Morny, the half-brother of Napoléon III) married Monsieur de Souza,
the Portuguese Ambassador to Paris.
As Minister of Foreign Affairs, the
Prince of Benevento had occasion again
and again to invite Monsieur de Souza
to dinner. At one of those dinners, an
awkward lackey caught the unfortunate
diplomat's wig on one of his cuff-
buttons as he was putting down a soup
plate in front of him.

" My peruke!... " groaned Monsieur
de Souza, whose head proved to be
completely bald.

" Don't take it out to the kitchen, "
Talleyrand ordered coolly, calling back
the lackey, " and let His Excellency
put on his peruke again before you
serve more soup. "

Talleyrand liked to surprise his guests by serving them rare and unusual food. During the winter of 1803 there was no fish to be had in Paris. On a certain evening, a few hours before a state dinner which Talleyrand was obliged to give in his mansion on the rue Saint-Florentin, the Minister learned that several of his guests had been saying:

" I bet they won't serve fish at Prince Talleyrand's. "

At the third course, a butler entered carrying a silver platter of unusual length on which lay an enormous salmon. Cries of enthusiasm from the guests, immediately followed by discreet groans: the butler stumbled and the coveted dish slipped from his hands. All eyes turned towards the master of the house.

" Have them bring in another salmon, " he said calmly, which was done immediately. The incident had been staged in advance.

BRILLAT-SAVARIN, AN UNINTERESTING GUEST

At Talleyrand's table, one frequently met an extremely tall personage with a heavy tread. Certain people—like Carême—thought he looked like a parish priest.

The guests who sat next to him at the table retained only a vague impression of him. The man spoke seldom and ate a lot. He did not seem to be witty. Sometimes he even fell asleep before dinner was over.

Appearances are deceiving. This unassuming man was secretly at work editing a book that was to make him a best seller among authors of French cookbooks. His book, *La Physiologie du Goût*, would be the Bible of genuine gastronomes, the chef-d'œuvre of the Science of Good Food, the most glorious monument to the Art of Good Eating.

Brillat-Savarin—B.S. to accomplished gastronomes—was born in 1755, at 62 Grande Rue, in Belley (Ain). His father, Marc Anthèlme, seigneur of the land of Pugière-en-Bugey, was public prosecutor in the local courts. Actually his name was simply Brillat. Savarin came to him through Mademoiselle Savarin, his great-aunt, who made him her sole legatee on condition that he would add Savarin to his surname.

Brillat-Savarin had two brothers: one became deputy public prosecutor at Belley, the other Colonel in the 134th regiment of the line. He also had three sisters: Marie and Gasparde, who remained unmarried, as did he. The youngest sister, Pierrette, had a complete repertoire of lusty songs and died at the dinner table, at the age of 99 years and 10 months, shouting to her servant:

BRILLAT-SAVARIN

" And now, girl, bring me the dessert! "

Brillat-Savarin—related to Madame Récamier—could have had a political career. Elected deputy to the Estates General, he became mayor of Belley four years later. But this man who was so clever in the kitchen knew little about binding the sauces of politics.

" A gastronome is always averse to the idea of a change in regimes, " said Henrion de Pansey.

B.S. most certainly was. He could not tolerate the new regime and he made the mistake of saying so aloud. To escape the Revolutionary Tribunal he was forced to go into exile.

He went first to Switzerland. Later on, in America he was obliged to play the violin on the streets in order to live. This Sherlock Holmes of French cuisine was also a good violinist. A music teacher of Belley, Monsieur Suard, had been his professor. On his

123

return to France, Brillat-Savarin invited the old musician to dinner. The latter succumbed (another one!) before the third course—he had eaten too much of the *Oreiller de la Belle Aurore*, a marvellous pâté " invented " by Brillat-Savarin which he dedicated to his mother, Aurore.

LOUIS XVI IS THE MURDERER OF BRILLAT-SAVARIN

The *Physiologie du Goût* appeared in the bookshops in October 1825. Though the first edition did not bear the name of the author, the book was an immediate success. After much talk and speculation, and much research it was finally discovered that this was the work of Jean-Anthèlme Brillat-Savarin, magistrate in the Supreme Court of Appeals. By then it was too late: Brillat-Savarin was dead.

Four months after the publication of his book, he had been obliged to represent the Supreme Court of Appeals in the Saint-Denis Basilica, at the first official commemorative ceremony of the death of Louis XVI. Though ill at the time, Brillat-Savarin dared not refuse.

" It is the first mass for a dead man, " he said to the first President, " and the last for a living man... "

That was on January 21, 1826. He caught a cold which developed into a serious illness. He died on February 2, leaving four verses in guise of a will:

I am going away—I am going far away—to a place from whence no man returns,

What does one do, what does one say, in that new realm?

As we never hear from there, no one has been able to tell us,

But I have done some good and can die in peace.

The *Physiologie du Goût* was printed at the author's expense. When the book proved to be a best seller, the publisher, Sautelet, offered to buy all rights from one of Brillat-Savarin's brothers—the Colonel—as well as from the other heirs.

" All right, " replied the officer. " And while you are about it, you might also rid us of this contraption! "

This " contraption " was B.S.'s violin. It was a Stradivarius. Sautelet did not buy it himself. He let one of his friends, Henri Roux, take advantage of the windfall. Roux paid—three thousand francs ($120)! As for the rights, the publisher obtained them for a thousand francs. A thousand francs in that day!... the price of a horse.

As a bonus the heirs also granted Sautelet all rights to the other works of Brillat-Savarin: an *Essai Historique et Critique sur le Duel* in particular, as well as a *Théorie Judiciaire* and a *Projet d'Economie Politique*. Also several fairly licentious tales which, for a long time, were read on the anniversary of the author's death in his country house at Vieu-en-Valmorey (Ain).

THE APHORISMS
OF BRILLAT-SAVARIN

One should read and reread the *Physiologie du Goût*. It is the best way to work up an appetite.

The author may perhaps be criticized for not being as brilliant as Grimod de la Reynière. The pedantic tone is sometimes annoying. There are, nevertheless, so many wise observations in this book, such love of good food, that it would be ungracious to dwell on the imperfections.

His aphorisms are still famous:

(1) Animals feed: man eats; only a man of wit knows how to dine.

(2) By making man eat to live, the Creator invites him to do so with appetite and rewards him with pleasure.

(3) The table is the only place where one is never bored during the first hour.

(4) The correct order of foods is to start with the heaviest and end with the lightest.

(5) The correct order of beverages is to start with the most temperate and end with the headiest.

(6) A dessert course without cheese is like a beautiful woman with one eye.

(7) To invite someone is to take charge of his happiness during the time he is under your roof.

RECIPES OF B.S. THAT MADE AN END OF A VIOLIN PROFESSOR

L'OREILLER DE LA BELLE AURORE   *PILLOW OF BELLE AURORE*

Take a cushion of veal, two red-legged partridges, the saddle of a hare, a chicken, a duck, half a pound of fillet of pork and two sweetbreads, scalded.

Divide those meats in fillets, about three or four inches wide, remove the skin with which they are covered and let them marinate for at least twelve hours in olive oil and three glasses of white wine vinegar; add two or three onions cut in rings, a bouquet of thyme, salt and pepper.

Prepare two stuffings: the first made of lean meats of veal, pork, bacon and ham; the second composed of livers of chicken, duck and partridge, bone marrow fat, mushrooms and black truffles.

All these various items, whose quantity must be in proportion to the amount of the pastry, should be chopped fine. To each of the stuffings, separately, add one egg and one or two spoonsful of panade *(in other words, bread crumbs cooked in beef bouillon and reduced to a smooth paste).*

Put about 4 1/4 cups of sieved flour in an earthenware pot, 2 teaspoons of salt, three whites of eggs, a tablespoon of butter, a small glass of good champagne and mix all together with a little lukewarm water.

When this pastry is well blended, smooth and consistent, place it on a floured pastry board. Dry the pastry, roll it out, fold it and roll it out again...several times.

In technical terms, the pastry sets; that is it loses its elasticity, becomes firm, resistant and can no longer be thinned down; you must then stop work and wait ten minutes. Begin again to roll out the pastry, stretching and folding it until the air, escaping from the little bubbles that are formed, makes it puff up.

Set the pastry aside for half an hour.

Have two pounds of fresh butter, washed, pressed, and drained (work it, if it is hard, to make it easy to handle). Reserve a third of this butter for the inside of the pastry, take half of the other two thirds and spread it over the whole surface of the pastry which you have stretched and enlarged to a thin sheet. That done, fold it in half lengthwise and the same way across its width ; stretch it again and add the second half of the butter proceeding as you did the first time, taking care, before each operation, to dust the board with flour.

Roll out the pastry, fold it twice and divide it into two equal parts, one to serve as the bottom of the pie and the other for the top.

On a linen cloth sprinkled with flour, roll out one of the two parts of the pie to about an inch and a half thickness and form it into a square the sides of which will be large enough to hold the amount of meat you are going to use.

Arrange the fillets of meats in ten or twelve rows, lengthwise, allowing to overlap on the four sides a strip of dough about seven to eight inches wide with which you will close the edges. Between the fillets, place some pieces of black truffles which you have peeled, some blanched pistachio nuts and several narrow strips of pink-fleshed ham.

Cover these meats with a light layer of the first stuffing of veal and pork. Begin again to make new rows of fillets of meats, intermingling them with sweetbreads cut in rounds ; add some black truffles and some pistachio nuts, but do not put in any ham. Finish with a layer of the second stuffing, composed of livers and black truffles. Then dot on all sides with pieces of butter which you have kept in reserve.

Form the second half of the dough into a square like the first half and cover the meats with it ; cut off the portion of this dough which extends beyond the meat, (so that the piece forming the base is wider) and, with a pastry brush, dampen that part with a little cold water.

Press the top layer of dough to the bottom layer letting it extend beyond the meats and, to strengthen it, place on the edges a border of dough which will be, so to speak, the lace on the pillow.

Twist up the rest of the bottom dough in a coil outside of the border. Gild it, using a chicken feather dipped in two eggs yolks thinned with cold water.

Make five round holes on the pie, one in the center and one near each of the four corners. Garnish with half a calling card rolled in the shape of a tube.

The pie should be prepared quite a while before it is put in the oven. Bake for two hours.

Eat it the day after it has been cooked (Lucien Tendret).

Fig. 16.

Hure de Sanglier.

Fig. 17.

Cochon de lait cuit à la broche.

Fig. 18.

Jambon cuit à la broche.

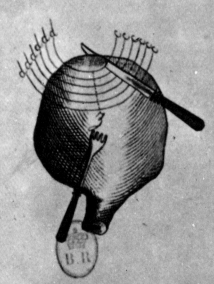

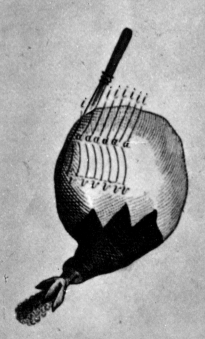

Fig. 19.

Jambon à la gelée.

Eleventh Course

SUGAR
IS INTRODUCED

On January 2, 1812, a prominent industrialist, Benjamin Delessert, received the following message:

" Urgent. Very urgent. To Monsieur Benjamin Delessert, Rue Coquevin.

" The Emperor is about to visit your factory. I am going there ahead of him. Come at once. "

The message was from Chaptal, the famous chemist who was also a Minister of the Emperor's.

Benjamin Delessert had recently shown the French that sugar could be extracted from beetroot for commercial purposes. For this feat the Emperor wished to thank him. Delessert, however, was not the inventor of the process. A Berliner of French origin, François Achard (1753-1821) revealed the secret in 1793, at Kunern, in Silesia, on the basis of researches made by the Prussian chemist, Sigismund Margraff.

Delessert was a man of importance. He belonged to an old Protestant family. It was his father, François Delessert, to whom Louis XVI entrusted several million francs for the purpose of reviving the silk industry.

Son of an influential father and provided with a comfortable inheritance, Benjamin was born in Lyon on February 14, 1773.

CARVER, BY BERNARDI *(Photo Josse Lalance)*

After leaving the artillery school at Meulan, he fought in the Belgium campaign with Pichegru and was then appointed aide-de-camp to General Kilmaine. After his return to civilian life, he headed a group of capitalists who agreed to make the First Consul a loan of 12 million francs to cover the deficit in the Public Treasury. At the time Delessert was only thirty years old. To show his gratitude Bonaparte made him head of the Bank of France, a post he was to hold for half a century.

Benjamin Delessert was also the founder of the savings bank; politically, he was Left of Center and as a member of Parliament worked hard at putting forward laws against gambling and lotteries.

We owe to him a very delightful " Guide to Happiness " (1804).

But to come back to our sugar.

Sugar began to be known in Europe at the start of the eighteenth century. The cultivation of the cane was introduced into Sicily before 1230 by Jews from Maghreb. Two centuries later, Spaniards planted sugar cane, first on Madeira, then in their colonies in America. Since then an important trade had developed between the Old World and the New. In those days sugar was considered a medicine. Colbert was the first to understand its importance as a basic food, and also to clap a special tax on it. It spurred him on to have France buy Martinique, Guadeloupe and a certain number of islands in the Lesser Antilles.

The first three refineries in Europe were set up in Rouen. Raw sugar was imported from America and transformed into *le sucre royal* or sugar candy.

BENJAMIN DELESSERT, THE FIRST SUGAR KING

No one knows how Margraff's discovery, perfected by Achard, came to the knowledge of the financier Delessert. Since 1808, the war with England, the Continental blockade, and a prohibitive tariff had virtually shut off all means of maritime commerce for France. Delessert, who was not as philanthropic as people say, saw the profit he would derive from documents and plans which a stranger offered him discreetly about the year 1809. He bought land in Passy and put up huge factories in which he installed the most modern equipment: his steam machines were among the very first. He also perfected certain methods of straining molasses and of crystallizing sugar. In short, he created the most modern industrial system of the age.

It was this factory, on Chaptal's advice, the Emperor decided to visit on January 2, 1812. Delessert was there to receive Napoléon. The Emperor inspected the project care-

INSPIRATION *(Photo Josse Lalance)*

fully and asked innumerable questions. He showed keen interest in beet sugar because he foresaw to what extent the product could become valuable, not only to his armies, but to all Frenchmen. The lesson the Emperor had learned a few years before, when the English had shamelessly taken over François Appert's discovery of food preservation through canning, was to work to the advantage of Benjamin Delessert.

At the end of the visit, Napoléon decorated the Passy industrialist with his own Cross of the Legion of Honor which he unpinned from his redingote. He even named him—on the spot and in front of his workers—a Baron of the Empire and he ordered his ministers to spare no means in developing the new industry rapidly. At his command special schools and more model factories were built. And finally he set aside vast stretches of land in the north of France to be devoted to raising beets.

Banker Delessert's sugar factory proved to be a gold mine: at the end of two years, his factories—all of them belonged to him—produced more than four million kilos of sugar.

But this golden age lasted only a short time. The fall of the Empire and the opening of maritime trade brought about a drop in the price of beet sugar. Colonial sugar refineries brought competition. The price of French sugar fell more than a third. Most of the factories went bankrupt.

132

PRINCE KURAKINE, AMBASSADOR AND GASTRONOME

At the time when Benjamin Delessert made it possible for Frenchmen to get along without colonial sugar, a Russian nobleman led them into modifying the arrangement of meals. He was the Czar's ambassador to Paris: Prince Alexander-Borisovitch Kurakine (1752-1812), grandson of Boris-Ivanovitch Kurakine who, a century before, had been the Talleyrand of Czarist diplomacy.

The event occured between 1810 and 1811. Up until then, it had been the custom in France to put everything on the table at the same time: entrées, chicken, roasts and vegetables. Everyone helped himself to whatever, and as much as, he pleased.

Prince Kurakine decided to do things differently in the bachelor's quarters of his Clichy manor-house. Nothing would be left on the table during the meal but the flowers and the desserts. As for the dishes, one or two servants would offer them to each guest, and then carry them back to the pantry.

This revolution in service set tongues wagging.

" At last, " people exclaimed, " we have equality at the table. All the guests are treated on the same footing. "

They called it eating *à la russe.* In less than two years all Paris was won over; in five years, all France. Never in all the history of French cuisine was a new fashion propagated so quickly.

After five years at the embassy, Prince Kurakine left Paris in 1812, the eve of the Russian campaign, which was to cost the French—among other things—fifty chefs, the most famous of whom was Laguipière.

Two years later the prince returned. After the abdication of Napoléon he accompanied the Czar to Paris to drink champagne with his Allies. He was one of the guests at the famous dinner given on March 31 by Talleyrand where arrangements were made to put the Comte de Provence on the throne. At dessert, the Count, although he was not present, was crowned Louis XVIII.

It was Antonin Carême who arranged that memorable banquet. He was then only the chef of the great of Paris. Talleyrand was to continue to take an interest in his career and to make him the chef of Kings—and the king of chefs.

It is time to introduce Carême.

Marc-Antoine—he was to call himself Antonin—was born in Paris on June 8, 1784. When he was eleven years old his father, a handy man, said to him:

" Go, my boy! In the world there are excellent callings. Leave us to languish! Misery is our lot and we must die of it. This is the day of splendid fortunes. It only needs wit —and you have it—to make one. Perhaps this evening or tomorrow some fine house will open its door to you. Go with what God has given you! "

It was a thin viaticum. But it made little difference. " Though born into one of the poorest families in France, " Carême writes in his Memoirs, " of a family of twenty-five children; although my father literally threw me into the street to save me, fortune quickly smiled upon me and a good fairy has often taken me by the hand to lead me to my goal. "

After wandering for several weeks around Paris, the boy found work and shelter in the household of the keeper of an eating house, where he remained four or five years. After that, through a lucky break, he entered the household of Bailly, the most celebrated caterer of the age, then living on the rue Vivienne. Carême had a flair for design and painting. His new patron advised him to go and improve himself with his leisure time at the print room of the Public Library.

" At seventeen, " writes Carême, " I was with M. Bailly, as his first pastry-cook. This good master took a lively interest in me. He allowed me to leave work in order to draw in the print room. When I had shown him that I had a particular vocation for his art, he entrusted me with the task of executing *pièces montées* (set pieces) for the Consul's table.

" I used my drawings and my nights

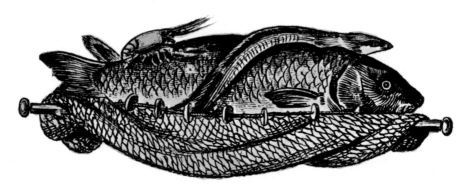

VIGNETTE DESIGNED BY CARÊME

in the service of M. Bailly. His kindness, it is true, rewarded my trouble. At his house I became an inventor. In those days the illustrious Avice, whose work taught me much, flourished in the realm of *pâtisserie*. Knowledge of his methods gave me courage. I did my best to follow him, but not to imitate him."

At the public library and at the print room Carême studied the five orders of architecture. Contrary to what might have happened, he did not desert his casseroles for the easel but applied his talents instead to making set pieces, the mere mention of which would, later on, make generations of *pâtissiers* dream.

"But," he confessed, "how many sleepless nights I spent before I reached that point! I could not give my attention to my drawings and calculations until after nine or ten at night! I would then work three quarters of the night."

It is difficult for a layman to imagine what a set piece by Antonin Carême was, at the time of the Consulate, and later under the Empire, when he himself was still working and was not content only to make sketches and be prodigal of orders and advice.

Certain set pieces prepared for state banquets covered several square yards. Sometimes they depicted a section of Paris in all its details and coloring, or a quarter in Versailles, or perhaps a country scene in the Ile-de-France. But more often it would be a monument or a site, which Carême created out of his imagination, and made of different pastries, of puff paste, preserved fruits, creams and sherbets.

Carême had no intention of going on just as a *pâtissier*: he was ambitious to be the monarch of the entire culinary empire.

THE BEST WERE
HIS MASTERS

Talleyrand himself urged him on. Not only did the Minister of Foreign Affairs order his state banquets through Bailly, but he borrowed the famous chef Avice twice a week. It was at the caterer's—and undoubtedly through Avice's mediation—that Talleyrand came to notice Antonin Carême.

Avice realized that Antonin Carême was full of ambition—and he took umbrage. All the more so as Carême no longer hesitated to criticize his superior, the *chef de cuisine*. Finally M. Bailly let the future " illustrious one " go to try his wings.

" If because of my age, " Carême was to write later on, " I do not have the advantage of being known as a pupil of the leading house of the old nobility (the house of Condé), I can at least say that I have been raised among men who bore a great reputation in those days.

" It was under M. Richaud, famous sauce-chef of the house of Condé, that I learned how to make sauces; it was at the state banquets given by the Hôtel de Ville of Paris and under the orders of M. Lasne that I learned the best recipes for cold dishes. At the Elysée Napoléon, under the auspices of Messieurs Robert and Laguipière I also learned, I venture to say, the elegance of the modern cuisine and the organic unity of a great administration. "

At last, the essential words:

" I have been constantly employed, since the rebirth of the Art, at dinners given by the Minister of Foreign Affairs and at the great banquets over the years. "

Undoubtedly, succeeding Avice, Carême was not employed in the Prince of Benevento's kitchens except at state dinners. Nevertheless, he benefited from the full protection of the Duc d'Otranto, whence the remark that is attributed to him: " One master: Talleyrand. One mistress: Cooking. "

HE IS ALWAYS
IN GOOD KITCHENS

But to return to Prince Kurakine whom we have left among the guests at that famous dinner of March 31, 1814, at Monsieur de Talleyrand's mansion on the rue Saint-Florentin. When the meal was over, his master,

Alexander I, motioned to him. The Czar had dined extremely well: he was pleased.

" I should like to have a French chef at my court in St. Petersburg, " he told his ambassador: " Attend to it for me, ' my little pigeon, ' " an expression Alexander I used for those of whom he was fond.

That was a mission of the greatest importance. The next day Kurakine approached Talleyrand.

" Do you think Carême would be willing to go abroad ? "

" Certainly. The proof: he is going to England in the next few days to enter the service of the Regent. But he will not be able to stand the climate very long. "

Prince Kurakine did not have time to reflect on Talleyrand's sibylline reply. A few months later he lost his mind as the result of wounds sustained during the fire at a ball given by Prince Schwarzenberg. He died in Weimar, June, 1818.

The diplomat would probably not have failed to make an arrangement with Carême. Just as Talleyrand predicted, Carême did not linger in London, and remained only a short time in the service of the future George IV, in fact—and this is significant—only until the meeting of the Congress of Vienna in 1815.

After that the chef of kings, again at Talleyrand's instigation, went to St. Petersburg. At that period Talleyrand had good reason to mis-trust the Czar. He had not forgotten the betrayal at Tilsit. He also knew that from now on Alexander was under the pernicious influence of a high-class adventuress: Baroness Krudener.

From then on Talleyrand and France were to have, in the very heart of the St. Petersburg Court and its intrigues, a secret informant—a spy in the uniform of a master-chef—who brought back, each time the plates were cleared, all the subjects discussed at the Czar's dinner parties.

From St. Petersburg, Carême went to the kitchens of the Emperor of Austria. He officiated at the Congresses of Aix-la-Chapelle, of Leybach and of Verona. Next we see him in the household of the Princess Bagration, then at Lord Stewart's and then in the bosom of high finance, the Baron de Rothschild's. And all those personages, all those places were of the utmost interest to Monsieur de Talleyrand.

Antonin Carême—to whom later on Louis XVIII granted the right to call himself " Carême de Paris "—was a spy. He is, however, above all else, the founder of *La Grande Cuisine Française*, classic French cooking as we still understand it today. If the French Revolution marked a break between the Old and the New Regime, it was Carême who turned the old regime of food into a new one. Thanks to him and his disciples, the monarchy was no sooner restored than the sovereignty of the French Cuisine

spread throughout all Europe. There was not a Court, not a manor, not a great house that did not insist upon having a " pupil of Carême's " in the kitchen.

Antonin Carême wrote several books which he published at his own expense. It was only later that he sold the rights to the unsold copies for the price of the paper, to Fayot, the publicist of the *Mémorial de Sainte-Hélène*. With the exceptions of Talleyrand (who paid him well and to whom he owed his career) and Laguipière (whom he was willing to recognize as his master because the latter died before he had time to quarrel with him and because he left no writing whatsoever) there are few indeed who escaped the sting of Carême's bitter pen.

" I strongly rejected those gloomy books that are the shame of our national cuisine, " he was to write bluntly. " I found them mediocre and full of errors. I have revenged the Science (of Cooking). "

Carême's own books are no less filled with epic pictures.

" The hour has come, to the minute, and we cannot delay serving. At that moment a man is beyond the extremes of exhaustion and suffering; he must obey even when he lacks the strength. Picture a great kitchen in which some twenty assistant-cooks are busy at their pressing tasks, coming and going, bustling about and each one in as great a hurry as the next! And all this takes place at top speed in that cauldron of heat where the man in charge must have a strong head and the ability of a great administrator. To add the last straw to our suffering, for almost half an hour doors and windows are shut so that the air will not chill the food. We can scarcely breathe: we are dripping with perspiration. "

Carême died—" burnt out by the flame of his genius and the heat of his ovens "—on January 12, 1833.

The Association of French Chefs recently found his grave, in Père-Lachaise.

TWO (SIMPLE) RECIPES OF CARÊME'S

VOL-AU-VENT   *PUFF-PIE*

1. *Make a flaky pastry which you roll out to a thickness of about 1/4 inch. Cut a round the size you wish the vol-au-vent to be ; with the rest of the dough line the sides and shape a cover for the top.*

2. *Your pie crust now being in shape, put it in the oven until it turns a beautiful golden color. From the inside remove the flakes of dough not thoroughly baked.*

3. *Then fill the inside with whatever mixture you please ; purée of chicken, purée of fish* à la béchamel. *Put the " lid " on your vol-au-vent and serve hot.*

LIÈVRE A LA ROYALE   *HARE A LA ROYALE*

There are at least a dozen recipes for lièvre à la royale. *Variations, often slight, are all that differentiate them. The one that follows is probably the most authentic : half a day is necessary for its preparation. Here then is the " monument " as Edmond Richardin reconstructed it according to Carême.*

1. *Skin and clean the hare. Set aside heart, liver and lungs. Very important : the blood must be carefully set aside.*

2. *Take a* daubière *(a braising pan) of adequate proportions with a tightly fitting lid. Grease it inside with goose fat. Spread on the bottom a layer of strips of salt pork and place on it the hare whose head you will have cut off. Cover the hare with another layer of sliced salt pork (there should be about 1 1/4 cups in all.)*

3. *Add a carrot cut in quarters, four onions stuck with cloves, twenty cloves of garlic, forty cloves of shallots ; a bouquet garni consisting of a bay leaf, a sprig of*

thyme and a few sprigs of parsley ; about a cup of red wine vinegar ; a bottle and a half of good Burgundy wine or Médoc that has been two years in the bottle ; salt and pepper.

4. Cover the braising pan and put it on the stove over a low, steady heat—without opening it—for three hours.

The first operation is finished. You have three hours before starting on the second part. Above all do not open the window during the cooking—this would change the temperature in the kitchen—and do not smoke. Don't forget that if Antonin Carême saw you make a single mistake, he would promptly throw you out. Now, during those three hours, you have a little job to do.

Chop separately one after the other ;

1. About 4 ounces of fresh pork fat 2. The heart, liver and lungs of the hare 3. Ten cloves of garlic 4. Twenty cloves of shallots. The garlic and shallots must be pounded and crushed fine. All having been chopped separately you now combine the whole carefully.

... Three hours have now passed. Take the braising pan off the stove, lift out the hare very carefully and put it on a hot dish. Sieve the contents of the pan through a colander into a bowl. Force the residue through with a pestle. To this broth add the forcemeat you have made and the remainder of the bottle of wine you used for the hare. Pour this new mixture into the pan and put the hare in again. Let it cook, always over a low heat, for another two hours. Then skim off as much fat as you can.

Finally, one hour later, while the hare is still cooking, skim off the fat once more. That done, cover tightly and prepare the blood which you will bind with the sauce a quarter of an hour before serving. Beat it a little so that no particle cakes, and pour it over the sauce, little by little, taking care to shake the pan gently back and forth so that the blood penetrates every corner. As to carving, do not worry ; the meat falls apart by itself.

THE MOST CELEBRATED GASTRONOMES GATHERED AT THE " ROCHER DE CANCALE "

(Photo.Josse Lalance)

Twelfth Course

A GOURMET KING
AND TWO MONARCHS
WITHOUT APPETITE

The Restoration!... the day of the great vogue for restaurants.

Since the Revolution, which had abolished corporations and privileges, restaurants had multiplied. They afforded every man an opportunity to enjoy, according to his purse or to his taste, the abundant or delicate meal, formerly the prerogative of the rich.

The refugees of yesterday were then in the full flush of their return to France. Louis XVIII helped them to forget the miseries of exile: he regilded their escutcheons and filled their purses.

The French bourgeois sported the white cockade, keeping the tricolor in the bottom of his pocket and of his heart. He learned to conjugate the verb " to stroll "—every hour and in all weather—up and down the boulevards.

St. Helena was too far away. The shadow of the Emperor no longer hovered over Paris and Paris hadn't a care in the world as it sat down to eat.

All Paris flocked to the *Café anglais* which the wine merchant Buret had recently opened with a magnificent dinner for the ten most famous gastronomes of the day. It cost him three *louis* a head (without the wine); for years to come hundreds of guests would insist upon having the same menu served them. The high light of that dinner was a famous soup which the *semainier* of the Opéra-Comique, Barthélemy Camerani, created in grattitude to Grimod de la Reynière for having dedicated his second *Almanach des Gourmands* to him. The basis of this soup is livers of chickens that must not be killed either by bleeding or by wringing their necks. In fact those chickens were the victims of the first culinary use of electricity. The flesh of chickens that have been electrocuted is said to have a very special flavor.

Equally popular was the *Café Bignon*, where Nibeau, successor to wealthy M. Pouillet, not only served dinner in his restaurant but also—an innovation that paid off—luncheon. *La Maison dorée* was also much frequented. There Hardy, the founder, had an excellent idea: on a grill installed in the main dining room, he had the famous *Rognon Hardy* (kidneys Hardy) cooked in front of the customer.

With their new fortunes and new social positions, and hungry for revelry, the *rentrants*, as the émigrés of yesterday were called, gathered at Véry's, in the Palais-Royal. There they were served naked girls on fish planks covered with a bed of parsley. But whether they had just returned from exile, or not, the gastronomes, the true gastronomes, preferred to meet at the *Rocher de Cancale*, run by Baleine. It was the most famous restaurant of the era, although the " illustrious "

Carême never missed an opportunity to run it down. Here lavish feasting was fashionable: it was even flaunted on the menu where the list of one hundred different dishes filled no less than three sheets. One of the waiters was famous: the regular customers nicknamed him " St. Vincent de Sole " because of his overweening trust. He lent them out of his own pocket the price of their bill (they called it in those days " *carte à payer* ").

" JEWELS " AND SCRAPS

The popularity of restaurants forced their proprietors to make serious strides in the culinary arts. They engaged genuine cooks who, under the Old Regime, would have found employ worthy of them only in the great houses.

In those days, a head chef in one of the leading establishments in Paris earned 4,000 francs in gold per year. The caterer in roast meats was paid 1,800, as much as the man who cooked the second course or the vegetable cook. The sauce-cook received 2,000 as did also the head pantry steward who occupied a trusted position. The scullions, the kitchen-boys, earned between 40 and 70 francs a week, but shared in the profits of the *bijou* (jewel).

What was the *bijou*? All the leavings from dishes and plates (fish, chicken, *pâtisserie*) which the kitchen helpers piled up in pails and sold for two to four francs, according to the quality of the leftovers. Those leavings were afterwards divided in two parts by their purchasers: the good parts were attractively arranged on platters and sold at the Saint-Honoré market. As for the " leavings of the leavings " they were made into scraps for use in making broths and were sold to owners of cheaper restaurants.

And finally, the lowest person in the kitchens and basements of the great restaurants: the dishwasher. His was the lowest of trades, constantly shut up in his *plonge*, a special room as hot as a Turkish bath, reeking with the odor of fats. The *plonge* had no windows so that the hot water would not get chilled (sic) and the dishes could be washed more thoroughly.

The dish and bottle-washer—the *plongeur*—did not earn any more than the kitchen helper. But he, too, had his *bijou*: he scraped up the layer of grease which formed on the surface of the dish water, skimmed it, and filled little kegs which could bring him in ten or twelve francs from the manufacturers of black soap.

Eugène Chavette—son of the famous restaurateur Vachette—declared that a qualified bottle-washer could fill as many as fourteen or fifteen kegs a month. Unfortunately he could not exercise his profession longer than two or three years: a human being's health has certain limits of resistance.

The first " soup kitchens " opened their doors towards 1830; they were cheap establishments where, for ten centimes one could get a portion of vegetables to eat on the spot, cooked in a broth made of scraps. The famous " Duval bouillons " did not appear in Paris until the reign of Napoléon III.

THE MURDERER A LA FOURCHETTE

The great Parisian restaurants had, of course, their regular customers and among them, some very eccentric persons. The most celebrated was the murderer *à la fourchette*.

His name was Gourier. Whether at the *Brébant*, at *Véfour*, at the *Café de Paris*, at *Tortoni's* or even at the *Café anglais*, all the *maîtres d'hôtels* knew him and spoke of him among themselves as " *le père Gourier.* " He was a rich land owner who secretly delighted in taking on one guest a year and eventually killing him...at the table. Rarely did the chosen victim hold out beyond the twelfth or thirteenth month of this " régime. " One evening, you would see Père Gourier appear in one of his customary restaurants accompanied by a new companion. The waiters would inquire anxiously about the former guest.

" I buried him this very morning, " the host would say tragically. Sometimes he would add: " I thought I'd get him before that... " Or else: " Pshaw! He was no great shakes! I got him in less than two months. " As for Père Gourier himself, he was in the best of health and he ate like a horse so that his guest would do the same. Chavette, who made a profound study of the subject, could not establish whether Gourier was done in by his seventh, eighth or ninth victim.

The " avenger " was named Ameline. His job: second assistant to the public executioner! Though his profession gave him plenty of leisure, it did not allow him to eat very well. Ameline was blessed with a tremendous appetite: people said he had " hollow legs " which served him as supplementary stomachs. The victims who had preceded him at Père Gourier's table had not been aware of what was in store for them. Ameline, however, knew— a *maître d'hôtel* or a waiter, perhaps seized with remorse, warned him.

Ameline gave no sign that he knew; but periodically he would disappear for two or three days, under some trumped-up excuse, to lighten his stomach (or stomachs) with a strong dose of castor oil.

One year passed. Then two. Almost every evening the two men dined together. In the end Gourier began to get nervous: never had any

of his victims held out so long. In vain he forced the heaviest dishes on him. Ameline helped himself as many as three or four times from each dish. He not only did not gain an ounce, but continued to enjoy the best of health.

" My whole fortune will be squandered, " Père Gourier said to himself: " but I'll get him as I did the others. "

He was mistaken. One evening at the *Cadran bleu*—an establishment considered the most expensive in Paris—Gourier was seen to turn scarlet, then white, when served with a fourteenth slice of sirloin. He threw back his head.

Ameline, seated opposite him, who had also just taken another helping of beef, thought Gourier was about to sneeze and playfully held up his napkin to protect himself. Gourier tried to straighten up. He managed a weak smile, but could not utter a word: this time, his head fell forward in his plate. Divine justice had struck down the murderer *à la fourchette*!

FROM THE LOVER OF SOUPS TO THE MAN WITH THE SAUCERS

Père Gourier was just one of the

regulars of restaurants—the race has become extinct, or almost—to enjoy a certain notoriety among the personnel. At the *Café Véfour*, waiters eagerly pointed out an amiable, pink-faced little old man, plump and charming, to whom it was wise not to suggest any red-blooded meat, or he would leave in a rage and never come back. In September 1792, this charming little man had carried the head of the Princesse de Lamballe all through Paris on the end of a spear.

At the *Café Riche*, one of the regular customers could not eat unless he had a pile of porcelain saucers beside him. He was completely bald and every now and then he would pick up one of the saucers and put it on his head. He claimed that was the way to ward off the cerebral congestion which threatened him.

Every month, at *Vachette's*, M. de Restac, the man who inspired Maupassant to write *Bel Ami*, arrived from his country estate. He would enter a dining room which he had specially reserved, and, seated in lonely grandeur, have himself served, one after the other, the forty different soups on the menu. This he invariably topped off with a meringue *à la crème*. He did not drink a drop of water.

At the *Café Philippe*, next door to *Rocher de Cancale*, another eccentric sent word once a month that he would come the next day and bring six friends to dine.

" You know them, " he would say, " they are all gastronomes... Well then: a louis a head and be sure the dinner is first-rate. "

The next day the man would arrive on the hour. He would express surprise that his guests had not yet come. He would wait for them a few minutes, cursing those rude people who could never be on time, not even for dinner. At last he would order the waiters to begin serving: his guests never came. He ate the entire meal he had ordered all by himself.

On certain evenings the habitués of the great Parisian restaurants went slumming. They visited establishments less select, in which they were " out of their element. " At *l'Académie*, for example, where each diner helped himself to one of the forty barrels set up in the main room, each cask bearing the name of a member of the French Academy and containing, of course, a different wine. When one of the " immortals " died, " his " cask was draped in black. No one used it again until another man of letters had been installed in the dead man's chair. That evening there was always a great celebration: only a certain number of the regular customers were admitted and the door was closed to all other clients. The wine of the new Academician was never the same as that of the dead man: that was where the surprise came in.

An atmosphere of youth, student

life and rowdiness was to be found principally at the *Rat mort*, avenue Frochot. And then, there was *La Vente libre*, where only women were admitted. The clientèle was composed chiefly of shopkeepers who sold costume jewelry and Paris fashions. Men, furious at being excluded, nicknamed the place *Le Ventre libre* (1).

A KING OF THE TABLE: LOUIS XVIII

Louis XVIII was a distinguished gastronome. He himself was a marvelous cook, and to him the culinary encyclopedia owes several recipes which he personally created. Somewhere in the archives of the House of France, there is a notebook in which the monarch entered with his own hand recipes and observations. In his tête-à-tête dinners with his friend Avary, the monarch tried out some unexpected recipes, for example:

La côtelette Louis XVIII (Cutlet Louis XVIII): Combine three cutlets which you put under the broiler: eat only the one in the middle which has taken all the juice from the other two.

―――――
(1)A play on the words *La Vente* (sale or bazaar) and *Le Ventre* (belly or womb). Impossible to translate. [Ed.]

146

Or else, l'*Ortolan Restauration* (Ortolan Restoration) which the king cooked with great care to satisfy the gourmet standards of his Minister of the Treasury, Baron Louis. His method took its inspiration from the preceding recipe: you take a dainty little ortolan and cook it in the stomach of a partridge which has been lined with foie gras and black truffles.

Louis XVIII said to Corvisart: " Doctor, gastronomy is disappearing and with it the last of the old civilization. Organized groups, like physicians, should make every effort to prevent society from breaking up this way. "

It was no surprise that Louis XVIII should have despised his brother, Louis XVI. The latter saw in a meal only a crude gesture of necessity. As Louis XVIII somewhat disdainfully observed: " My brother eats the way he takes his wife. "

A WAR CORRESPONDENT SETS THE FASHION FOR COUSCOUS *IN PARIS*

It was Charles X who brought back into fashion royal dining in public. Once a week he and his family sat down in a huge banquet room and

The " bœuf a la mode " restaurant *(Photo Josse Lalance)*

anyone could come to watch them at their meal. Frequently one of the guests would recognize someone he knew among the gaping onlookers; he would then call him over and offer him delicately, on the end of his fork, a piece of whatever he was eating. They called that " sharing the king's repast. "

But, while courtiers and idlers flocked to watch the royal family eat, two trout fishermen in the Vosges accomplished much more for the fame of French Cuisine. Remy and Gamin discovered the method of artificially fertilizing and hatching trout's eggs. After five years of research their method was perfected and " artificial " trout—considered at that time to be much better than " natural " trout—filled the markets. A scholar even went so far as to declare that the fish of MM. Gamin and Remy had the advantage over " real " (sic) fish because the former did not cause nettle rash.

Charles X—a stupid monarch—showed scant interest in that culinary revolution. He was too busy undoing and opposing his predecessor's admirable restoration policies. If he was preoccupied by any revolution, it was the revolution of the " Trois Glorieuses " which he was zealously preparing and which would leave him a hated outcast, in exile.

Aside from the vogue for restaurants, his reign would have no connection with this history had it not been for the conquest of Algiers. Maréchal de Bourmont, who commanded the expeditionary forces, was joined by the historiographer and playwright Jean-Toussaint Merle. Merle was a best-selling author of the time. His sentimental affairs—before he married the actress Marie Dorval—kept the gossips busy. For a long time he was the lover of an actress of sorts who was fairly unknown but not without talent: Léonide Valerie. She was Italian by birth and saddled with an enormous family which she had to support.

Merle was in the habit of meeting Léonide when the play was over. He then would take her to the *Café Vachette* or some other fashionable restaurant. Once seated, he did not order a sumptuous dinner like most of the other customers, but, simply, some rice pudding. Léonide and Merle were well known Parisian personalities and their passion for rice pudding was soon talked about. They were promptly imitated, to the point where certain restaurants of the day—the *Véfour* for instance—listed on their menu Rice Pudding *à la Toussaint Merle*. With the years, the name became *Riz de la Toussaint* (All Saint's Rice) and was served traditionally, up until the war of 1914, on November 1st (All Saint's Day).

Attached to de Bourmont's general staff—as a sort of war correspondent—Merle sent to the newspapers of the day articles whose variety further increased his notoriety. In one of his " Letters from Algeria, " he explained to the French people for the first time what *Couscous* was. Other writers followed suit and, aided by current events, a number of Parisian establishments carried *Couscous* regularly on their menu.

LOUIS-PHILIPPE EATS LIKE A CHEAP-JACK

In his own right, Louis-Philippe is of no more interest to a history of the evolution of French cuisine than was his predecessor, Charles X. When he was a little boy, he asked his governess (Madame de Genlis):

" What is a bull ? "

" He is the father of the calf. "

" What is a cow ? "

" She is the mother of the calf. "

" And what is the ox ? "

Madame de Genlis almost choked. Then, being a woman of wit, she said: " He is... the calf's uncle. "

Having become " King of the middle-class French, " Louis-Philippe remained fairly eclectic in his relations. The dining room at the Tuileries was open to all. The wood panelings concealed secret mechanisms by which the portraits on the walls could be " automatically " changed. When the monarch entertained a courtier of the old nobility at dinner, he was surrounded by portraits of Louis XVI and Marie-Antoinette. But the canvases were double-faced: a mere pressure on a button and the pictures of several figures of the Revolution appeared.

At the dinner table, following the custom of all bourgeois houses of the day, the son of Philippe Egalité carved the chicken himself with great skill, dividing the pieces among his guests. The king was fundamentally economical and his entourage no less so. The regular caterers to the Tuileries lost a lot of business. Louis Philippe inaugurated a system of dining at a fixed price, based on the importance of his guests. To lessen his housekeeping expenses he even cut down on his kitchen staff. Every morning he specified:

" Tonight I am entertaining the Belgian ambassador... Important: serve six dinners at ten francs. " Or: " Tonight, we have no one of any importance... two dinners at 3 francs will do. "

IN FUTURE ASK FOR A " MONTMIREIL A LA BÉARNAISE "

Gastronomy did not lose its impetus during the reign of that stingy bourgeois king who was also a coward. He was to lose his throne with a senile imbecility that surprises us even today. His flight from Paris was like that of a thief—or better still, an " impostor "—he didn't even take time to carry off in his carriage, crammed with linens, china and silver, a single basket of food.

At that period, thanks to Carême and his pupils and disciples, the French had become acquainted with the cuisine we know today. With the development of railroads they were able to eat fresher fish, sea food and fresh vegetables. Thanks also to scientific discoveries the breeding of animals was making progress and the animals were healthier. As a result meat gained in quality and greater quantities were consumed.

After 1840 bread was no longer just a mixture of various cereals and potato flour. Yeast was now added to the dough. The kneading machine was widely used and stoves, which up to then had been heated only by wood, now burned coal.

M. de Chateaubriand was a peer of France, but he was not the father (*le père*) of the fillet of beef which has helped to popularize his name. It was his chef—Montmireil—who first had the idea of cutting a thick slice from the middle of the fillet, broiling it, garnishing it with potatoes cut in large cloves, cooked in butter and served accompanied by a sauce *béarnaise*—so called not because the recipe originated in Béarn, but because it had been prepared for the first time in the kitchens of a restaurant in Saint-Germain-en-Laye, the Pavillon Henri IV. And in that, Montmireil was merely observing the tradition of great cooks: he did not give his own name to " his " culinary discovery, but dedicated it in the name of his master.

TWO NOURISHING RECIPES

POTAGE CAMERANI   *SOUP CAMERANI*

*Scald and blanch separately and in the amount according to the number of guests:
some celery, cabbage, carrots, turnips and leeks. Drain and chop all very fine. Put
the vegetables in a casserole with a large piece of butter, some salt and pepper and let
them simmer over a low heat. A few minutes before they are done, mix in some chicken
livers, also chopped very fine. (Important note: allow ten livers per guest; the chickens
must not have been killed either by wringing their necks or by bleeding.)*

*Meanwhile scald, cook and drain some macaroni. Grate some Parmesan cheese.
Then take a heat-proof soup-tureen and butter the bottom inside. Make a layer of
macaroni, then a layer of forcemeat, ending with a layer of grated Parmesan cheese
dotted with butter. Begin again in the same order, first macaroni, then forcemeat,
then cheese and build the layers up to the edge of the soup-tureen, taking care to finish
with a layer of cheese. Put the soup-tureen over low heat. Let it simmer and serve
(Baron Brisse).*

LE COUSCOUS   *COUSCOUS*

*There are as many ways of preparing couscous as there are of preparing cassoulet,
beef bourguignon, civet of hare and other regional dishes. The classic recipe is the one
prepared by our friend, Paul Levillain, one of the best gastronomes of our day.*

*For four persons: 1/2 pound of a special crushed grain (semolina) known as couscous;
a small chicken or half a fowl; one pound of shoulder of mutton, 1/4 pound of chick-
peas, 3 carrots, 2 turnips, 3 tomatoes, a little vegetable marrow, the heart of a small
cabbage. A little aniseed, some fennel, 1/4 pound of butter, 2 tablespoons of olive oil,
13 little cayenne red peppers.*

(Note: Chick-peas must be soaked in cold water 12 hours before using.)

*Recipe: 1. Cut the meat of mutton and chicken into small pieces. In a fairly deep
earthenware pot sauté them in 4 soupspoonsful of butter, adding 3 or 4 minced sweet
red peppers. Cook it all together till golden brown and salt lightly.*

*2. Pour hot water over the meat, enough to fill the pot three-quarters full; add the
chick-peas, carrots and turnips minced, 1 tomato peeled and cut in pieces, the vegetable
marrow peeled and diced, onions, cabbage, a pinch of cayenne red pepper, aniseed*

and fennel. Let it boil, skim it as you do for pot-au-feu *and cook it gently for 3 hours with the pot covered.*

3.   *Now put the couscous into an ordinary colander and run cold water over it to soften it thoroughly, then spread it out on a dish-cloth and let it swell for 15 to 20 minutes.*

4.   *Then take a colander that fits into your pot, but be sure that the bottom does not touch the boiling broth.   The Arabs use a* keske, *a special ustensil with holes through which only the steam from the liquid can reach the couscous.   An enamel colander will do.*

5.   *Take the lid off the pot and in its place cover the pot with a damp cloth, set the colander on this cloth and pour the couscous into it; cover tightly with the lid of the pot and let it cook over moderate heat for 20 minutes.*

6.   *After this first cooking, work the couscous carefully with your fingers to break up any lumps, then moisten very lightly with a little broth; return it to the colander which should still be on the cloth covering the pot in which the meat is cooking—it should be almost done.   Let the couscous steam for another 20 minutes.   At that time, test it to see if it is done; if it still seems too firm, begin the preceding operation over again, but the semolina must not be a purée.   The grains must stand out separately, one from the other.*

7.   *While this last cooking is going on, prepare separately 2 sauces; mince a sweet red pepper and 2 peeled and seeded tomatoes.   Let the vegetables brown in 2 tablespoons of butter; and steam them over a low heat until done (30 to 35 minutes).*

8.   *Meanwhile cut and peel 2 cayenne red peppers, cook them in olive oil; after a few minutes remove from the fire and keep hot.*

9.   *When the couscous is done, turn it into a very hot, deep dish, mix with it the rest of the butter divided into little pieces (about 1/8 pound of butter in all).   Mix with a fork to separate the kernels thoroughly without crushing them.   Keep hot.*

10.   *Strain the meat and vegetables and arrange them on a hot platter.*

11.   *Moisten each of the two sauces with a soup-ladle full of broth in which the meat was cooked.   Stir each preparation well and serve in separate sauce-boats.*

The couscous may be served garnished with meat and vegetables, but it is preferable to serve them separately.   Each guest takes what he pleases, being careful not to crush the semolina uselessly.   The sauces are, in any case, always served separately.   Red pepper, sweet or hot, is put on the table at the disposal of the guests.   N.B.   The use of vegetable marrow and peppers is optional.

DINNER IN HONOR OF SAINT-HUBERT, PATRON SAINT OF HUNTERS, AT THE VÉFOUR IN 1844

ALEXANDRE DUMAS PÈRE *(Photo Josse Lalance)*

Thirteenth Course

WHEN THE FATHER
OF THE
THREE MUSKETEERS
DINES

In 1869, Alexandre Dumas père announced that he was going to " spill the beans. " He was old and tired. A long journey across Russia and a number of crowning excesses had at last physically exhausted that indefatigable writer, whose work includes over three hundred volumes.

" I intend, " he declared, " that my last work shall be a cookbook composed of memories and desires; a book whose learning and wit will not frighten the practical cook and will perhaps merit reading by serious men and not-so-serious women whose fingers will not be too wearied in turning the pages. "

Six months later, the manuscript of the *Grand Dictionnaire de la Cuisine*— a huge work of some two thousand pages— was in the hands of Alphonse Lemercier, publisher and friend of Dumas. The débâcle at Sedan was to delay the publication of this volume for three years. Dumas would not even have a chance to read the proofs of his last volume. He was to die—a pitiful invalid, completely paralysed—in the midst of the tragic decline of the Second Empire, a few weeks before the siege of Paris.

" This is a big child I had when I was quite little, " his son was to say as he lifted him into a first-class carriage of the Western Railway to take him to his property on the sea-shore where the author of *The Three Musketeers* said he wanted to die.

EVERYTHING IS READY WHEN MADEMOISELLE MARS ARRIVES

Dumas was as great an eater as he was a story teller. The idea of writing a cookbook had haunted him for twenty years.

" It will be my last work, " he declared, " the one I shall outline the moment I catch a glimpse of Death on the horizon. "

His gastronomic education had been long and detailed. It began when he was twenty-four years old and enjoying his first successes. He was then divid-ing his time between the cozy inti-macy of Mademoiselle Mars, one of the queens of the *Théatre des boulevards*, and the sensual and ardent favors of Mademoiselle George. The latter's patron was Frédéric Harel, manager of the Odéon theatre where she herself was an actress. Through Dumas, Harel had made a fortune out of the productions of " Christine, " " Richard Darlington, " " La Tour de Nesle. "

In the end manager and author fell out, perhaps because of Mademoiselle George. Harel was to die in an insane asylum.

" You eat too much, " Harel said to Dumas.

" Man doesn't live on what he eats but on what he digests, " replied the latter.

When Dumas went to Mademoiselle Mars' for supper it was the night for Almond Soup (*Soupe aux amandes*). When, after the theatre, he escorted Mademoiselle George back to her apartment on the rue de l'Ouest, that was the evening for " Truffle Salad " (*Salade de truffes*).

Mademoiselle Mars lived on the rue de la Tour-des-Dames. At her house the food was excellent and dainty. No sooner did Julienne, the actress's housekeeper-cook, hear the door of her mistress's " ramshackle conveyance " slam than she rushed to her stove to give the last touches to that famous almond soup. Dumas would take three platesful of it... before he started on turbot, pheasant or guinea-hen, quail or partridge. Everything was ready. After she had blanched the almonds Julienne removed the skins: but often she tossed the almonds into a mortar and, after sprinkling them with water to prevent them from drying out, pounded and crushed them. Then just before the guests went to the table, she poured boiling water over that very smooth paste, strained it all through a very fine cloth and added hot milk to it.

" Mademoiselle Mars, " Dumas relates, " has just time enough to slip into something comfortable and I to unlace my boots surreptitiously, for my feet always hurt me, especially when I am at table (sic). "

MADEMOISELLE GEORGE PEELS THE TRUFFLES HERSELF

The evenings consecrated to Mademoiselle George and her truffles were quite different. The food on the rue de l'Ouest was not as famous as at Mademoiselle Mars'. In his memoirs, Dumas even went so far as to say that certain dishes served in the household of Frédéric Harel's protégée were " like incendiary fire-boats. "

That belated statement did not in the least prevent our good man from confessing, a few lines farther on, that Mademoiselle George had a " very different knowledge " from Mademoiselle Mars'. Mademoiselle George did not require any of her servants to wait up for her return from the Odéon. Dumas took her home; she went in ahead of him and immediately lighted all the lamps. Then she began to undress without any false modesty, even when people who were not close friends were present. Walking back and forth from one room to another, she talked about everything under the sun, criticizing her theatrical colleagues and other kept actresses in particular—whose protectors she always insisted had been at her feet the day before. During that interlude, Dumas père unlaced his boots, always surreptitiously, of course. Then they went into the dining-room where a luxuriously appointed table was already laid. In the very center stood a huge gold and silver bowl filled to overflowing with five or six pounds of truffles, whose priceless scent perfumed the air and assailed their nostrils as they entered the room.

The mistress of the house then began to peel the truffles, using a silver knife reserved solely for that purpose. She seasoned them with milk of almonds, wine, champagne or liqueur as the mood seized her. Then followed pâtés, aspics or chicken and various other cold dishes that one of the guests, under Mademoiselle George's instructions, would fetch, all prepared, from a table in the pantry. To wind up this love-feast, Dumas was generally asked to prepare a salad " in his own style, " the famous *Salade à la Dumas* for which he was to give us the recipe in writing:

SALAD A LA
ALEXANDRE DUMAS PÈRE

" You must know that Monsieur
Chaptal, the chemist, is the first in
France to have had the idea of satu-
rating salad with oil, salt and pepper
before adding vinegar to it. For it is a
fundamental error to believe that
pepper and salt dissolve in vinegar...
In the Chaptal method therefore, we
have the double advantage of distrib-
uting the salt and the pepper more
evenly, and of collecting the excess
vinegar in the bottom of the salad
bowl.

" Now that we know this, here is
my method: I place the yolk of one
hard-boiled egg for each two persons
in a salad-bowl. I moisten it with oil
and crush it to make a paste of it...
To this paste I add a little chervil,
some minced tarragon, some ground
anchovies, some chopped gherkins and
the whites of hard-boiled eggs also
chopped fine. Salt and pepper.

" Over it all I sprinkle a good
vinegar, then I put the lettuce in the
salad bowl. At this point I summon a
servant to toss the salad. When he has
finished, I drop a pinch of paprika on

THE GARRET ROOM

MAURIN

it from a good height. It is now ready
to be served. "

DUVAL
SUPPLIED THE MEAT

About 1844, Dumas père was seized
with remorse: he regretted having
given up those wonderful suppers
" at home "—restaurants were then
the vogue—where there were always
such wit and high spirits. He made up
his mind to give, each week, a dinner
for fifteen to which he invited, every
Wednesday at eleven o'clock at night,
his best friends.

" All I ask of you, " he explained
to each of his guests, " when you
cannot come, is that you inform me
far enough in advance so that I can
provide for someone to replace you that
night. "

Most of the guests belonged to the
theatrical world. That was why he
chose to give a supper rather than a
dinner; eleven o'clock instead of seven
o'clock.

159

" And also, " he confided, " because
I have noticed that supper is as far
removed from the business of the day
before as from the business of the next
day. The mind is therefore completely
free; there are few things which, if they
have not been done before midnight,
can be done after two o'clock in the
morning. " As for the menu: a soup,
a pie made from some game, a roast,
a salad. Duval—of the " Bouillons "—
supplied the meat.

Duval had not yet launched his
" chain " of cheap restaurants. A
butcher in a rich section of Paris, he
complained that he sold only the good
pieces of meat whereas the others were
left in his meat stall. A few years
later, on the advice of Dr Véron (of
whom we shall speak in a little while),
Duval copied the formula of the
" Dutch Broths " (*Bouillons hollandais*)
and perfected it. He was taking a great
risk as the dish had had scant success.
He opened a shop first on the rue
Montesquieu where he sold his combination of boiled beef, broth and
vegetables. He was soon to add to that
menu and it was not long before his
" broths " (*Bouillons*) were to multiply
throughout Paris. In order to keep
his prices down, Duval dispensed with
tablecloths and napkins. His customers sat at marble-topped tables, on
chairs that were purposely uncom-
fortable to discourage them from
lingering.

" But how do you manage not to
lose money with such low prices? "

he was asked. Duval smiled: " I earn
very little on each dish, of course, "
he explained, " but as the portions are
not large, a diner, who does not want
to go away hungry, is really obliged
to get ' seconds. ' The result is that,
without noticing it, he ends by paying
as much for his meal as he would in a
first-class restaurant. "

Alexandre Dumas' weekly suppers
continued for two years. It was about
that time that *The Three Musketeers*
appeared (serialized in *Le Siècle*). And
at the same time the first gas stoves
appeared in bourgeois houses.

THE END OF ROMANTIC KITCHENS

They were discussed from one end
of Paris to the other. Soon the most
renowned gastronomes raised their
voices in praise of this discovery. One
of them, Roger de Beauvoir, did not
hesitate to call it " a new constel-
lation. " And he explained:

" The concentrated furnace invented
by the author of the gas-stove is
worthy of description. It is a sort of
case of iron and grillwork in which a
double row of gas jets is arranged

160

opposite the food to be roasted. The food is subjected to the action of those thousand tongues of fire, exposed to them, cooked and recooked and is presented to the consumer in all its splendor.

" A more material advantage the gas stove offers is that the kitchen will occupy little space in future private houses. A stove as large as a mahogany or rosewood dressing table will satisfy the needs of four meals if, like our good ancestors, we still indulge in four. "

Those " little iron boxes, " which domesticated gas, saw the era of the stoves with the multiple fires (which all private homes and all mastercooks were so proud of) disappear. It marked the end of those romantic kitchens of which Victor Hugo spoke with emotion at the middle of the nineteenth century.

" At Sainte-Menehoulde I have seen a fine sight, the kitchen of the *Hôtel de Metz*.

" This is a real kitchen. An immense room with the chimney in the middle, an enormous cavern filled with a splendid fire. On the ceiling a black network of magnificent smoke-encrusted beams from which hang all kinds of delectable things, baskets, lamps, a meat-safe, and in the center a large open-work net from which vast pieces of bacon are suspended.

" The glowing hearth shoots beams of light into all the corners, cuts out great shadows on the ceiling, casts a fresh rose tint on the blue faience, and makes the fantastic edifice of pans glow like a wall of fire. If I were Homer or Rabelais I would say: ' This kitchen is a world and this chimney is the sun. ' "

Is there even one of those " dream kitchens " still in existence in which simmered and crackled and bubbled all those dishes which today are the pride of French cooking?

ADMIRABLE SOPHIE, DR. VÉRON'S COOK

When Dumas was not working—which was fairly rare—he was to be found most often at the *Café Riche*, managed by Louis Bignon, one of the greatest restaurateurs of the nineteenth century. All the illustrious personages, all the famous artists and great writers frequented Bignon's café on the corner of the rue de la Chaussée d'Antin and the Boulevard des Italiens. It was without doubt the most famous house in Paris: its reputation was world-wide.

There *Sole à la Riche*, *Bécasse à la Riche* (Woodcook *à la Riche*) and many other dishes which even today figure prominently on the menus of all restaurants of international fame, were cooked to perfection under Bignon's observing eye. Bignon was the first French restaurateur to be decorated with the Legion of Honor: *chevalier* in 1867, *officier* in 1878.

At the Café Riche, Dumas père met all the men he liked: Sainte-Beuve, Flaubert, the manager of the Opéra, Nestor Roqueplan, and the manager of the Opéra-Comique, Dr. Véron, with his official mistress, the marvelous actress, Rachel. Dumas was very fond of Véron, undoubtedly because he was greatly indebted to him. The latter, also a newspaper man and even a newspaper editor (the *Constitutionnel* under the Second Empire), was the first to serialize novels and print them in his newspaper. He invented the famous formula " to be continued in the next issue. " Viel-Castel, a suspicious and bitter man, has left an ugly portrait of Dr. Véron:

" He is a fat man, with no neck, a bloated head, flabby cheeks, a pug nose, a protruding stomach... He is called *le prince de gale.* " (Le prince de Galles = Wales; gale = mange or itch).

True, Véron was fat, to be sure—like all *bons vivants*—but he had exquisite charm. French cuisine owes much to him: he was one of the most lavish hosts in its history. While numerous other hosts entertained at their own expense once or twice a week, Véron gave himself the luxury of a dinner *daily* at his house, with about thirty permanent guests. Some of them came back every night—except Friday— even when they had not received a formal invitation. They were the " pensioners " as Véron called them and whenever they appeared he would order another place set and urge his guests to move a bit closer.

" I ask only one thing of you, " the master of the house explained to his guests, " that you always have at my table as much wit as good humor. "

Dr. Véron lived on the rue de Rivoli. As his numerous occupations gave him little time to linger over preparations for his dinners, he relied completely on his housekeeper whom everyone called Sophie (her name was really Victoire Delalande) and whose food the gourmets of that day praised to the skies. Sophie was a Norman. She had first worked for the dancer, Fanny Elsler, who " gave " her to Dr. Véron out of gratitude for a delicate service he had rendered her. Sophie stayed with him thirty-five years.

" Sophie is the only woman to whom I grant the right to bear the title of ' cook, ' " Alexandre Dumas père was to say of her.

Always dressed in black, her hair completely covered with one of those caps with deep fluting that servants wore, Sophie never allowed a valet to enter " her " gentleman's bedroom. She herself helped her master to dress and watched over the details of his wardrobe. It was Sophie who opened the door and took upon herself to welcome—in her fashion and according to her good will—or to dismiss the caller. Among all of Véron's friends, her favorites were Achille Fould, the Minister of Finances whom she considered " most distinguished ", and Sainte-Beuve, because he amused himself by inviting her to the restaurant. But she never forgave the latter for being named senator, an honor " her " gentleman never obtained.

Through Dr. Véron's guests, Sophie's personality attained a fame which is hard to account for today. It was nevertheless so and Véron showed with pride the letters his cook received... either asking for her advice (not always on culinary matters) or making her wonderful offers. Prince Napoléon-Jérôme and the duc de Mornay both brought pressure to bear on Véron again and again to obtain Sophie's services.

" But, my good friends, " Véron replied very bluntly, " she would kill you at table. " And pointing to his enormous and prominent paunch: " Come now! Do you see yourselves with a ' thing ' like that? "

THE HOST OWED HIS FORTUNE TO A CHEST SALVE

Dumas père, Sainte-Beuve, Nestor

Roqueplan, Arsène Houssaye, the composers Aubert and Fromental Halévy, and Adolphe Adam were among the most assiduous guests in Dr. Véron's dining room. They frequently met there two physicians whose fame was soon to extend beyond the borders of France: Trousseau and Velpeau.

Véron had a secretary, Malitourne, a busybody, who liked to pass himself off as the power behind the throne in that household. There was also a master of ceremonies—of whom Sophie was jealous—Comte Gilbert de Voisin, husband of the celebrated dancer, Taglioni. Voisin was an agreeable and charming man but dangerous when he needed money—which was frequently.

To prevent his dinners from becoming monotonous, Véron sometimes invited a few women too. They were never of high society, but courtesans who made no effort to hide their profession. The Friday dinner was in actual fact reserved. That day, the old friends knew they would not be admitted to the table unless they had received a formal invitation. It was the only day when strict ceremony was observed at Dr. Véron's table. It is true that the guests were always important political personalities: the Prince-Président was often one of the guests. In other respects everything was very simple, but in keeping with the most elementary rules of courtesy and good taste. Each guest was free to get up from the table when he pleased or when his occupations demanded. But it was the host himself who was often the first to rise. Every evening he attended a dress rehearsal and he was never known to arrive after the curtain went up.

Dr. Véron was a very rich man. How otherwise could he have kept up his role of amphitryon? But he did not owe his fortune to his position as manager of the Opéra-comique and even less as the editor of a newspaper. He owed it to a pharmaceutical specialty—the Regnauld salve to relieve the chest. Véron did not invent it: he had bought the formula from one of his former Faculty colleagues. It was he in any case who launched the product in a style that was much criticized in his day and which was dubbed " revolutionary. " He was the first to apply publicity to other things than books, in other words, to make consumer products equally profitable.

Véron died unhappy. Not poor and abandoned, but because he was obliged —for reasons of health—to give up his dinners and his various other activities. When, after his death, it was announced that the contents of his cellar would be put up for sale, many people imagined they would find there the most famous and most respectable brands. They were mistaken. The " modern Trimalchio, " as Véron was called, had not given any banquets for several years. The auctioneer had only bottles of mineral water to offer at the public sale.

A few years later all the guests of the Véron dinners met again at Père Lachaise. The dead man's body was exhumed and moved to another grave. It was Sophie, rich in years, fame and *embonpoint*, who had the charming idea of sending out the invitations on " cards " exactly like those formerly used to invite the celebrities of Paris to dinner.

164

RECIPES FROM DUMAS PÈRE

LANGUES DE LAPINS DE GARENNE   *WILD RABBITS' TONGUES*

1. *For six persons allow sixty tongues of wild rabbits. Scald, cool and skin them.*

2. *Make a mirepoix. Add the tongues. Moisten with a tablespoonful of consommé, a glass of Madeira wine, and half a glass of white wine. Add a few nice truffles. Cover the cocotte with waxed paper and braise it over low heat.*

3. *Half an hour later, take out the tongues. Set them aside. Pass the stock (in the pot) through a sieve: add a good sauce espagnole and let it reduce. Strain it through cheesecloth and return the tongues to the sauce. Decorate with quenelles of chicken and strips of truffles. Sprinkle with the juice of a lemon and reheat over a bain-marie.*

HOMARD A LA PORTOS   *LOBSTER A LA PORTOS*

1. *Brown in butter two onions and three carrots finely chopped, some thyme and parsley.*

2. *Cut a live lobster in pieces: cook it with spices, a bottle of extra-dry champagne, 1/8 pound of butter and some red pepper. Cook half an hour and serve hot.*

ÉCREVISSES A LA D'ARTAGNAN   *CRAYFISH D'ARTAGNAN*

1. *Plunge two dozen live crayfish (for four people) into about two and a half quarts of salted boiling water. They are cooked when they turn red. Drain. Set aside the little claws, the ends of the large claws and the tail.*

2. *In a large casserole put a little over one quart of meat broth to which you have added shallots and chopped parsley. Add the crayfish, let them cook five minutes; bind with the yolks of two eggs; dot with about 1/5 of a pound of butter and the juice of one lemon. Serve the crayfish with plenty of the hot sauce heaped over.*

OVER CAPABLE OF ROASTING OVER ONE HUNDRED CHICKENS, ABOUT 1860

(*Photo Josse Lalance*)

Fourteenth Course

BARON BRISSE
IS NOT A HORSEMAN

On February 6, 1855, two hundred prominent men were invited to a banquet that was to be a landmark in the history of French cuisine. For the first time in Paris and in France, horsemeat was to be eaten officially.

At the Grand Hôtel that evening only one hundred and thirty-two guests showed up. Sixty-eight persons therefore had declined the invitation: some on false pretexts, others declaring bluntly that to eat a horse would "seem to them like eating a man." The celebrated naturalist, Geoffroy Saint-Hilaire, presided. Among the guests: Quatrefages de Bréau, member of the *Institut* and well-known naturalist; A. Richard and Du Cantal, directors of the *Jardin des Plantes et d'Acclimatation* ; the lawyer Desmeret, mayor of the 3rd *arrondissement;* M. Decroix, an influential member of the Society for the Protection of Animals. Also a few writers: Sainte-Beuve, Alexandre Dumas père, Charles Monselet, Gustave Flaubert, Dr. Véron, Jules Janin...

The Grand Hôtel, which had opened its doors in 1852, was fashionable and impressive; most of the official receptions were held there. The master-cook was Balzac (no relation to the novelist) to whom French cuisine owes several famous dishes, among others,

L'omelette norvégienne (Norwegian omelet). Here, therefore, is the menu of the first banquet of horsemeat.

Soup: vermicelli in horsemeat broth. Hors d'œuvre: sausages and roast horsemeat. Meat dishes: boiled horsemeat, horsemeat *à la mode*, ragoût of horsemeat, fillet of horsemeat with mushrooms. Vegetables: potatoes fried in horsemeat fat; salad with oil of horsemeat. Dessert: Rum and horse marrow cake.

Quatrefages de Bréau gave the customary toast: "I thank you all for coming here this evening without any prejudices and for leaving with the conviction that horse is as good to eat as beef."

In the course of the following months, three butchershops selling horsemeat opened in the poorer quarters of Saint-Marceau and Popincourt. The year after, on July 8, 1856, a banquet similar to the one held at the Grand Hôtel, was organized in the center of Paris in the Lemardelay butchershop. And eventually, a cheap restaurant in the Latin Quarter selling horsemeat dishes was opened for students.

BARON BRISSE AND HIS THREE HUNDRED AND SIXTY-SIX MENUS

That evening in 1855 a "very Parisian" personage refused to attend the banquet at the Grand Hôtel: Baron Léon Brisse. His absence gave rise to numerous and varied comments.

Ildefonse-Léon Brisse was born in Gémenos, near Marseille, in 1803. He would undoubtedly have made an honorable career in the Department of Waters and Forests if an affair of honor had not compelled him to give up his post as master of the wolf-hunt and drastically altered his social position. He turned to journalism and specialized in articles on gastronomy. From 1855 on, he was the author most in vogue on the subject. Five years later he reached the apogee of his career when he brought out, in *La Liberté*, the first daily column on cooking. Thanks to him the circulation of *La Liberté* increased, forcing the other papers to print recipes and gastronomic items also.

Brisse had, unfortunately, neither the erudition of Grimod de la Reynière nor the philosophy of Brillat-Savarin. Although he did not know how to cook, he was a master in the Art of the Table.

His explanations are sometimes rather ludicrous.

"In my opinion," he declared, "the disappearance of hot *hors d'œuvres* from bourgeois menus is the result of the excessive development of women's skirts. Don't misunderstand me: in a well organized house, the over-expenditures on one side have to be balanced by economy on the other."

His intimate friends were never sure

that Brisse was not trying to pull off an e-nor-mous joke that would insure success for his next article. Enormous? He himself was enormous, for that matter. Every morning and every evening, in the coach that ran from Paris to Fontenay-aux-Roses where he lived, two places were reserved for him alone. He took great delight in exaggerating his bulk: every day he arrived at his office with his pockets bulging with various foods. When the pockets were full, he used his hat, cramming into it, helterskelter, everything he had craved en route: foie gras, pickled herring, truffles, etc.

BRISSE MISSES HIS LAST DINNER

Not all of his colleagues liked him. They envied his success, his air of happiness. They were jealous of him for being entertained by men of renown. They did not forgive him for having a table set apart for him everywhere.

"Baron," they twitted him, "your guts smell of burnt fat!"

In 1872, Brisse slipped on a banana skin (sic) and broke his leg. From then on he settled permanently at Fontenay-aux-Roses, in the house of his landlady Gigout, with whom he shared the family table. The old sybarite's retreat was quickly discovered: Fontenay-aux-Roses and the Gigout inn became a favorite place of pilgrimage for the gourmets of the day. To be sure, the food was not always first-rate—it depended on "Maman" Gigout's mood—but if the Master was in good form a man was certain to be well repaid for his trouble. Sometimes Brisse remained in the dining room for as long as a day or two, carousing with old "cronies" who had come specially from Paris: "Baron" Page, Roger de Beauvoir, Jules Gouffé, the composer Rossini whom Brisse had persuaded to marry his cook, and Charles Monselet, his heir-apparent in culinary journalism.

The honor of dying like Grimod de la Reynière, to which Idlefonse-Léon Brisse aspired, was denied him, although he missed it by only a few hours. On June 13, 1876, feeling his end approaching—he was 73 years old—he invited six of his old friends to a last dinner. As the hour drew near for his visitors to arrive, the old man asked his landlady Gigout to help him to his bedroom to make ready for them. Once there, he asked to be left alone. "Maman" Gigout went back to her pantry. The guests arrived. As there was no sign of their host, they went to look for him: they found him dead. After a moment of stunned silence, Monselet suggested:

169

"Let's go to the table anyway. He never liked stews overdone."

For several years, on the eve of that anniversary, the same six friends gathered at Gigout's to share the same menu, the table set with a seventh symbolic place: Brisse's.

AT NOHANT, THE MOST ATTRACTIVE DINING ROOM IN THE WORLD

After the catastrophe of Sedan, the King of Prussia's cook served, during a luncheon which brought William I and Napoléon III together again, Donkey's Brains à la diplomate (Cervelle d'âne à la diplomate). The insult to the Prince-Président was not justified. For nearly twenty years, thanks to him, France knew a gay and pleasant period, in the course of which the French were out of touch with world affairs. They had no recourse but to busy themselves with their own affairs.

A first-rate cook was perhaps what the sovereign lacked most, for he was not the "somnambulistic dilettante" whom George Sand talked about. He liked to have a good time, but he knew very little about pleasures —those of the table in particular. But never, under any regime, would the French have so many facilities for eating well, so much taste for exquisite dining. If there is a Golden Age of the French cuisine, it was certainly during the Second Empire. The extraordinary vogue for restaurants, even more frequented than during the Restoration, attested to that alone.

The craze for the art of Good Eating was reflected in most of the literary works of the day. Re-read the details of Madame Bovary's wedding feast and you will be hungry. As for Dumas, he brought to a close a production of three hundred volumes (in which the hero seldom did penance)... with a cookbook. Pick up the short stories of Mérimée, or else Capitaine Fracasse by Théophile Gautier: the mountebanks just dream of Pantagruelian meals. Review the dramatic criticisms of Saint-Beuve or of Janin: they never missed a chance to regret one of those chickens roasted to perfection... when they had sat through a flop, or four, which also means oven.

And finally re-read the Journal of the Goncourts, the Souvenirs of Maxime du Camp: every twenty pages your appetite will be aroused. If you travel through le Berry, do not fail to visit George Sand's house at Nohant, where you will see the most appetizing dining room in the world. Musset and Chopin dined there with other celebrities. Even when they had lost the

ADVERTISEMENT FOR A COOKBOOK, ABOUT 1850 *(Photo Josse Lalance)*

lady's favors, they would never lose the honor of dining with her.

SAINTE-BEUVE : THE GOOD FRIDAY SCANDAL

"Rejoice, my little stomach," said Sainte-Beuve, "everything I earn is for you."

He was the habitual guest of Dr. Véron and was very much at home in all the restaurants. If he was not particular as to the quality of his conquests, he was precise, meticulous and an experienced connoisseur in all matters concerning the table. He ignored the fast days. A free-thinker and *provocateur*, he never failed to organize banquets on Good Friday. The one on April 10, 1868 overstepped all bounds and caused a veritable scandal.

At dinner with the critic of the *Lundis*: Prince Napoléon, Taine, Edmond About, Flaubert, Renan and Robin, of the *Académie des Sciences*. On the menu: Tapioca Soup, Salmon-trout; Fillet in Madeira wine; Pheasant stuffed with truffles; Baked crayfish; Asparagus tips; Salad; Café parfait; Dessert. Wines of the best years: Château-Margaux, Nuits, Musigny, Château-Yquem, Champagne.

Newspapers published reports of the dinner; and the incident took on alarming proportions. The Church made it an affair of State because of the personalities of Sainte-Beuve and his guests. The writer was obliged to come up with an excuse for his colleagues:

"It was the only day Prince Napoléon was free!"

Rossini, the composer, did not yield the palm to Sainte-Beuve in any way. He had married his cook and spent every leisure moment perfecting a machine for making macaroni. He squandered his fortune on it. "God! how boring fame is!" he declared... "The pork butchers are the happy fellows."

"You should have been one."

"Of course, I would have liked that... But I was so ill advised!"

In any case, we owe to Rossini the invention of the *Tournedos* to which, from then on, his name would be affixed. It all happened at the *Café Anglais*, one evening when Rossini declared he was "tired of the everlasting piece of beef listed on every menu."

"Take something else."

"No, I don't like anything but beef."

He then gave instructions for the meat to be prepared in another way. The *maître d'hôtel* gave a sudden start:

"Never would I dare to offer a thing as... unpresentable."

"Well! Then arrange not to let it be seen."

From then on, when a client ordered a Tournedos *à la Rossini* it was not served before his eyes, but... behind his back. Whence the name: *"tourne le dos"* (turn one's back).

A FEW OF THE BARON BRISSE'S RECIPES

TERRINE DE FOIE GRAS   *TERRINE DE FOIE GRAS*

Take a goose liver weighing between a pound and a quarter to a pound and a half. Dice one pound of calf's liver and three quarters of a pound of pork fat; melt the fat on a low fire, add the minced calf's liver and season the whole with salt, pepper, spices and chopped bayleaf. Put this mixture over a high heat for not more than four minutes, stirring it with a wooden spoon; cool it, pound it and press it through a sieve. This done, peel two or three truffles, an equal number of fine shallots and insert four or five pieces in the liver.

Put a layer of the mixture in the bottom of an earthenware pot, of suitable size, lay the liver on it, surrounding it with several slices of truffles, garnish the sides and then cover it with the mixture. And top it off with a layer of pork fat and one bayleaf.

Cook over a bain-marie *on low heat. Be sure to keep the water boiling constantly but do not let it touch the pot. It should be cooked in an hour and a half; to be sure, test the contents in the pot with a larding needle which, when you take it out, should be boiling hot. Cool, cover the top of the pot with lard and chill.*

COCHON DE LAIT EN MARCASSIN   *SUCKLING PIG EN MARCASSIN*

Take a large suckling pig with a black head; smother it. With the help of a funnel, pour into its snout a burning hot concoction of thyme, bayleaf, basil, sage and rosemary, which has been boiled in water for half an hour and strained through a sieve. Tie the snout, stretch the animal out on a plank and leave it there over night so that it will be completely impregnated with the perfume of the aromatics.

The next day, skin it like a hare, leaving the bristles around the tail and the head. Clean out the insides; singe it over hot coals, lard it with bacon, marinate for twenty-four hours in vinegar with parsley, thyme, bayleaf, slices of onions and carrots. Turn it several times during this interval.

To roast it, wrap it in waxed paper, put it on the spit and cook it at medium heat; remove the paper a few seconds before you take the animal off the spit to let it brown and when it is nicely browned remove it from the spit, arrange it on a platter and "mask" it with a sauce poivrade (pepper sauce) to which you have added the juices skimmed from the dripping pan.

LA GARBURE   GARBURE

Cut up a cabbage in quarters, blanch it, squeeze it between your hands to get all the water out of it; tie each quarter and place them in a casserole in which you have put a layer of bards of lean bacon, with some pickled pork, a few slices of ham, a veal knuckle and some left over boiled beef, if you have any. Add carrots, onions and a bouquet garni. Add another layer of bacon and cover with water. Simmer over a low heat for at least two hours.

When it is done, simmer some slices of bread in the broth, take out the cabbage quarters and remove the strings. Then take a buttered oven-proof soup-tureen and sprinkle with grated cheese. Arrange on the bottom a layer of cabbage covered with a bed of Gruyère and Parmesan cheese grated together and on top of that a layer of the bread (simmered in broth) also covered with a layer of cheese; begin again with a layer of cabbage, then a layer of cheese until the tureen is filled. End with a layer of cabbage heavily sprinkled with cheese. This operation completed, put the tureen under the broiler for a few minutes and serve.

The meat — pork, ham, veal — is usually served as a separate course.

Première année. — N° 1.   20 CENTIMES   Dimanche 21 Février

LE GOURMET

Parait tous les **Dimanches**

———

ABONNEMENT

PARIS		DÉPARTEMENTS
n.... 12 fr. »		Un an.... 14 fr. »
ois.. 6 fr. 50 c.		Six mois.. 7 fr. 50 c.

BUREAUX

5, *Rue Coq-Héron*, 5.

———

de la ligne : Faits Paris, 5 fr. — Réclames.
3 fr. — Anglaises et Affiches, 1 fr.

LE GOURM

Parait tous les Di

ABONNEM

PARIS	DÉ
Un an.... 12 fr. »	Un a
Six mois.. 6 fr. 50 c.	Six

BUREAUX

5, *Rue Coq-Hér*

Prix de la ligne : Faits Paris, 5
3 fr. — Anglaises et Affi

LE GOURMET

JOURNAL DES INTÉRÊTS GASTRONOMIQUES

RÉDACTEUR EN CHEF : M. CHARLES MONSELET.

INVITATION A LA TABLE

I

l'année dernière, en terminant une étude sur Grimod

» La gastronomie est la joie de toutes les situations et
de tous les âges.

» Elle donne la beauté et l'esprit.

» Elle saupoudre d'étincelles d'or l'humide azur de nos
prunelles ; elle imprime à nos lèvres le ton du corail ardent ; elle chasse nos cheveux en arrière ; elle fait trem-
bler d'intelligence nos narines.

III

C'est une profonde erreur de croire qu
humble condition, — et même le pauvre
participer aux jouissances de la cuisine. I
telle hérésie, il faut n'avoir jamais péné

Fifteenth Course

CHARLES MONSELET,
THE GASTRONOME
WITH THE CLUB-FOOT

With the Baron Brisse gone, Pierre-Charles Monselet (1825-1888) stepped easily into the official role of Prince of Gastronomes. Stoutish and pink-cheeked, he looked like a merry and worldly cleric who had put on secular garb. His reputation as a gastronome added to his popularity; his avocation of gourmet lent his writings a note of particular originality.

Monselet was born, with a club-foot, on April 30, 1825, in Nantes, at the corner of the Place Graslin and the rue Jean-Jacques Rousseau.

On June 19, 1846 the *Lafitte-et-Gaillard* stage coach set Charles Monselet down in Paris. Limping, already growing stout, he put up at a little hotel on the rue du Mail and if his lips did not actually utter Rastignac's words " *A nous deux Paris,* " Monselet certainly thought them. Aside from several letters of recommendation to various newspaper managers he was rich only in hopes. For a long time he led a Bohemian existence, living by his wits, using every expedient to keep from starving to death.

Monselet was, however, an indefatigable worker. His literary output was tremendous. Today we would call him a "*pisse-copie*." In addition to articles, notes on Paris and theater reviews, which he sent regularly to two or three newspapers and to as many magazines, he soon had a successful play on the Boulevards. Several of his novels were published. On his work table, *L'Histoire du Tribunal révolutionnaire* was in the process of being finished.

He began to earn a little money. In 1852 a new magazine, *Le Monde Illustré*, appeared. And Monselet was the drama critic at fifty centimes a line. At the same time, Sainte-Beuve and Jules Janin—both older than Monselet and both much more famous —were receiving only thirty centimes a line, the former on the *Constitutionnel*, the latter on the *Journal des Débats*.

In spite of his infirmity, Monselet fought two duels: one with Émile Augier (two shots with no result) the other with Théodore Barrière who wounded him in the hand with the point of his sword. The official report of the second duel was drawn up by two constables. Cost: a fine of two hundred francs for Monselet and of one hundred francs for his adversary.

But the hobby of this man of all trades was gastronomy. His greatest pleasure was to dine with a group of devoted friends. He praised the merits of Good Food in verse and in prose: and his verses (of which we give a sample) are among the best that have been composed on cuisine.

Sonnet du potage

« Lorsqu'il fallut dîner dans cette auberge
[atroce,
Le front de mon ami se rembrunit soudain.
On mit notre couvert dans le fond du jardin,
Près d'un jeu de tonneau dilosqué... Quelle noce !

Le potage manque totalement d'attrait.
Un lac d'une blondeur terne — rempli d'alarme.
Mon ami s'écria : « Quel bouillon !... Il faudrait
Pour lui percer les yeux un fameux maître
[d'armes !...

Je ne l'écoutais pas. Mon caprice suivait
La fillette, au jupon rouge, qui nous servait :
Opulente beauté ; seize ans et du corsage !

Et j'allais répétant : « Vois donc quels yeux,
[mon cher !
Lui, tout à son idée et d'un accent amer :
« Que n'a-t-elle jeté ses yeux dans le potage !»

HE FORGETS ÉMILIE FOR THE PLEASURES OF THE TABLE

Monselet wrote a lot on cooking. Aside from his *Almanach des Gourmets* which appeared every year for five years and in which sonnets and prose alternated pleasantly, one should read his *Lettres gourmandes* addressed to Émilie, a charming love of his youth.

" Ah! Émilie! " he exclaims in the first letter, "How I loved you!... But now I love ortolans' thighs and a bottle of Château-Palmer."

Read his "table talks," one of which is devoted to his "spiritual father," Grimod de la Reynière. At the end he writes: "All controlled and rational passion becomes Art: and, more than any other passion, gastronomy is capable of being rationalized and controlled.

"Think this over carefully: the most charming hours of our life are all connected—by a more or less tangible hyphen—with a memory of the table.

"Gastronomy adds joy to all situations and all ages. It provides beauty and wit; it provides gentleness and politeness."

And you must read *La Cuisinière poétique*, a work in which several of his faithful friends collaborated: Alexandre Dumas père contributed his recipe for roasting chicken on the string; Duranty discussed the boudin of Lille and Mèry praised in alexandrines the seasoning of Bouillabaisse.

During the winter of 1858, a friend of Monselet's, M. de Saint-Léon, suggested that he start a gastronomic newspaper.

"All right," exclaimed Monselet : "We'll call it *Le Gourmet*."

The dinner to inaugurate *Le Gourmet*, which Charles Monselet gave on February 25, 1858 in the salons of the Hôtel du Louvre, is still famous. Among the guests: Théophile Gautier, Nadar, Nadaud, H. de Villemesant, Arsène Houssaye, Henri Murger, and Aurélien Scholl.

This is the menu of Monselet's dinner, classic in type.

Soups: *Soupe à la Duchesse. Soupe à la Saint-Georges.*

Second Course: Salmon *à la vénitienne.* Turbot with oyster sauce. Fillet of beef *à la royale.* Ham *à la macédoine.*

Entrées: Gourmet's swallows' nests. Breaded lamb chops with asparagus tips. Timbale of rice *à la siamoise.* Mayonnaise of embellished lobsters. Sparkling sherbet. Roman punch.

Roasts: Truffled chicken. Barded woodcocks. Galantine of pheasant. Truffles in Madeira wine.

Vegetables: Asparagus. Petits pois Victoria.

Dessert: Fruit cup *à la parisienne.* Charlotte *mousquetaire.* Jelly *cardinal.* Bombe *surprise.* Fruit.

As for Wines: First course: Madeira brought from the Indies; Clos Saint-Estèphe; Hermitage blanc, *grand cru;* Château-Paline 1846: Crémant. Second course: Xérès Aboccado; Château Laroze 1841; Château Lafitte 1847; Clos Vougeot; Veuve Cliquot; Porto Vieux.

CHARLES MONSELET RECOMMENDED THESE RECIPES

BOUILLABAISSE   *BOUILLABAISSE*

1. *Take 5 pounds in all of the following fish (or of some of them) : Saint-Pierre, rascasse, red mullet, whiting, gurnet, spiny lobster, crabs... Wash them, clean them, and cut them in good sized pieces.*

2. *Take a good earthenware pot—as large as possible—and fill it up to a third with a good olive oil mixed with a quart of water.*

3. *Toss the fish into the pot with a cup of minced onions, 2 1/2 tablespoons of chopped parsley, 2 bay leaves, 2 cinnamon sticks, 1 sprig of thyme, 2 cloves of garlic not peeled, about 2 tablespoons of shallots, 4 slices of carrots, about 1 tablespoon of salt, 1 teaspoon of pepper and 3 tablespoons of sweet red peppers. Add a spoonful of saffron to color it; let it boil, stirring constantly for several minutes.*

4. *Decant into a soup tureen part of this marvellous broth to which you add some croutons of well fried bread. Serve the fish separately.*

POT-AU-FEU   *POT-AU-FEU*

Put 2 pounds of beef, a piece of veal knuckle, a ham bone or the remains of a roast chicken in a pot. Add two and one-half quarts of cold water and put your pot on a low fire so that the water—heating little by little—can gradually dilate the fibres of the meat and dissolve the gelatin in the bones and nerves.

Skim the fat off gently and add a little salt, two carrots, a turnip, an onion stuck with a clove, a sprig of celery and two leeks.

Complete this seasoning with half a clove of garlic or a little grated nutmeg.

Let the pot boil again and then simmer gently, without interruption, for five hours. Then take out the vegetables and the meat. Skim and pour the broth on sliced bread which has been browned in the oven. The broth must always be very lightly salted (Le Gourmet, April 18, 1858).

THE KITCHENS OF THE CHÂTEAU DES TUILERIES *(Photo Josse Lalance)*

Sixteenth Course

A FRENCHMAN
INVENTS MARGARINE

On July 17, 1869, a man of medium height, with graying hair, wearing spectacles, entered the doors of the Imperial Society of Inventions and Researches. He had already been there a week before and had deposited a document of some fifty sheets of closely written pages. An employee told him to come back in a week in order to give "those gentlemen" time to study what the visitor claimed was a "revolutionary discovery."

The examiners of requests for patents read the document attentively. They felt, furthermore, that there was something interesting in it and they bestowed on the document belonging to the engineer, Mège-Mouriès, the number 86,480. They had registered the discovery of margarine.

One year before, Napoléon III had opened a competition from which it was hoped to find a product, both rich and edible, and having more lasting qualities than butter, with which to supply the crews of the Imperial navy.

The contest was not an inspiring one for researchers: there was one participant only: the recipient of the patent, Mège-Mouriès, in the economic services of the Department of Agriculture.

As soon as he learned of the discovery, Napoléon III personally congratulated the engineer. He promised to help him put it on the market. He did not have time... The Prince-Président's mind became preoccupied with the oncoming conflict which, in a few months, would erase the twenty years of prosperity he had given the French.

A METHOD
FOR TRANSFORMING
MARGARINE INTO BUTTER

Some time before the war of 1870 Mège-Mouriès managed to set up a factory at Poissy for exploiting his discovery. It ran only a short time. He was obliged to close it and wait for better days. Taking advantage of the enforced delay he began to search for a method that would transform margarine into butter and on May 11, 1874, he took out a new patent.

"I have only," he explained, "to churn my margarine with a specially prepared mixture of cream and milk and a dash of butter to obtain the taste of sweet cream from the farms. By then smoothing out the mass obtained after churning, I can get a product which, in addition to the taste, has the consistency of butter and can be used exactly like butter."

This was too much! Two years before, in 1872, the Board of Health had intervened. The worried producers of butter entered a complaint against the ambitious Mège-Mouriès who wanted to launch his "economical butter" on a grand scale. The Board decided to authorize the sale of margarine on the express condition that it should not be labeled as butter.

"It is obligatory," they decided, "for packages of margarine to have a cubic shape to differentiate them from packages of butter. They must bear the word margarine printed on all four sides, with no other designation than a commercial mark or the name of the manufacturer (1)."

THE ACADEMY
OF SCIENCES
AGAINST MARGARINE

When the producers of butter learned that Mège-Mouriès had a new device for calling his margarine "butter," there was another uproar. Complaints poured into the Ministers' tables and even to the President of the Board. The agricultural engineer had foreseen those reactions. His counter-attacks were at

(1) In principle this law is still in effect in France.

184

least as virulent as his adversaries' offensives. But he had to fight on two fronts at one time. First against the butter manufacturers, who were ready for an all-out struggle; and then against a second front formed by all the foreign competitors who had organized and had obtained patents for products inspired by his invention. In addition to his patent in Paris, Mège-Mouriès had taken out one in England and thought he would be sufficiently protected. In this he was mistaken: in America and in Germany he was widely plagiarized.

Mège-Mouriès held out for four years. Then the blow fell. On May 11, 1880, influenced by a change in the political atmosphere, the Academy of Sciences declared itself opposed "to the utilization of margarine in the kitchens of public establishments." In their report they mentioned particularly:

"Margarine contains a much greater quantity of fatty acids than does butter: this proportion is too strong for the fat to be completely emulsified and for the organism to be able to absorb it. That deficient assimilation could have a bad effect on the bodily equilibrium.

"In addition there is nothing to insure that the margarine manufacturers always use fully guaranteed materials. Even if the health officers are very strict with the manufacturers there can never be sufficient control in the country." Sole concession: "that margarine may be utilized for certain stews and vegetables, but never, at any rate, for cooking potatoes."

That report, as one can imagine, had considerable repercussions. The butter makers were triumphant. The consumption of margarine, in France, fell off immediately.

RAT MEAT?...
WHY, IT'S VERY GOOD!

The ancestor of *steak à la Bordelaise* is *steak à la Tonnelier*. It is made with rats fattened in the wine-making plants of the Gironde. After they have been cleaned and singed, covered with a light layer of oil and a lot of coarsely chopped shallots, they are grilled on a fire made from the remains of casks or vineshoots.

The gourmets who have had an opportunity of eating rat—after overcoming their prejudices — declare that, when the animal has been well fed, the flesh is delicious. It is said to have a slightly musky taste that is not unpleasant.

Parisians, forced to eat rat during the one hundred and thirty-five days of the siege of Paris in 1870-1871, did not all share that opinion. And the fact of having "eaten rat" remained in the memories of the Paris citizens

185

as the symbol of their most serious humiliation.

There are many reports on life in Paris during the siege. The winter was harsh. Shopkeepers had nothing to sell, although they managed to make money hand over fist. In December 1870, a box of sardines cost 5 francs, butter 50 francs the pound, an egg 2 francs, a cat 10 francs, a rat 3 francs, an apple 60 centimes. As for the rat, the newspaper *Le Temps* recommended "submitting the meat to prolonged cooking to destroy harmful germs."

CAT
IS A FINE TIDBIT,
BUT DOG IS TOUGH

"Towards the end of December 1870, we had the greatest difficulty making up menus that were fairly 'suitable,' " declared the famous chef, Thomas Génin (he died in 1887).

"There was scarcely anything to be had but horse. Beef and veal had long since disappeared. Mutton had been replaced by dog which was sold by chicken dealers, and rats were substituted for young rabbits. Cat was considered a rare tidbit. The rat was repulsive to the touch but its flesh of tremendous quality: delicate but not too insipid. Well seasoned, it is perfect.

"I have served grilled rats as 'pigeons *à la crapaudine*' but more often as potted meat, with a stuffing of donkey's meat and fat. I called that terrine of rats *à la Parisienne*. A terrine of rats cost fifteen francs.

"Donkey was rare: it cost 15 to 20 francs a pound. Donkey meat has a slight taste of hazel nuts: it cannot be compared to horse meat. As roast beef, with beans *à la Bretagne*, it is a real treat. The quality of the mule is somewhere between the donkey and the horse.

"Dog meat is tough. It has a disagreeable taste which all the spices in the world cannot disguise.

"As for the meat of billy-goat," Thomas Génin winds up, "I have a very definite opinion about that. The Culinary Art will never succeed in making it an edible dish. I have used oxalic acid, tartaric acid, nitric acid, sulphuric acid... It is impossible to get rid of the odor."

It was not goat that was eaten on New Year's Eve, December 31, 1870, at the famous restaurant Noel Peter's, *Passage des Princes* To celebrate his recent appointment the new Mayor of the 3rd *arrondissement*, M. Bonvalet, gave a dinner for twenty people. He had been one of the people who suggested killing the animals in the Zoo to feed the sick in hospitals and old people in almshouses. As he had connections in high places, he was able to help

CAT AND DOG MEAT ON SALE DURING THE SIEGE OF PARIS IN 1870
(Photo Josse Lalance)

Fraysse—the proprietor of the restaurant—by obtaining a few supplies and by making out the menu which would be served at his table on New Year's Eve. *Hors-d'œuvre*: sardines, celery, butter, olives. *Soup:* Sago *au vin de Bordeaux. Second Course:* Salmon *à la Berzelus. Entrée: Escalope d'éléphant,* with shallots sauce. *Roast:* bear *à la sauce Toussenel. Dessert:* Apples and Pears.

HE DEDICATES HIS COOKING TO THE VIRGIN AND INVENTS LOBSTER A L'AMÉRICAINE

Reculet was in command of the kitchens of Noel Peter's restaurant during the siege of Paris. Before that, he had been in the service of the Comtesse d'Auteroche. He had made a certain name for himself as author of a cookbook—a book of more than 500 pages—whose only touch of originality was that it was dedicated to the Virgin. On the first page of the *Cuisinier Pratique* we read:

"Because, O Holy Mother, you are spotless and the model of most perfect, most immaculate purity, I place under your holy protection the future of a work that treats of a science to which propriety is so fitting."

It is not impossible that M. Reculet was also the man who invented *Homard à l'Américaine* (Lobster *à l'Américaine*). A mystery continues concerning the identity of the creator of that excellent dish. Escoffier thought it had been imported to America by a chef from Nice. On the other hand, most culinary authors state positively that this dish was served for the first time in Noel Peter's: Fraysse, the proprietor, is supposed to have given it that name in honor of some customer from across the Atlantic (1).

---

(1) Others think that the recipe for *Homard à l'Américaine* originated in Brittany and that it would be correct to say *Homard à l'armoricaine.*

188

SOME RECIPES UTILIZING ANIMALS FROM THE ZOO

CRÉPINETTES DE GROS GIBIER   BIG GAME SAUSAGES

Chop up forty pounds of hippopotamus, rhinoceros, wild boar, wart hog or aardvark meat. Add ten pounds of fat, an eighth of a quart of sugar, a tablespoonful of ginger, an eighth of a quart of pepper, one pound of salt, a tablespoon of oregano, three tablespoons of savory.

Combine and mix well and run it three times through a meat chopper. Place all in a sterilized jar. Cover with a heavy layer of hippopotamus fat. Keep in a cool place.

To cook it, toss it in boiling fat and wait until the collops are well crusted on both sides. To garnish a chicken, combine the flat sausage meat with an equal amount of thick paste made of flour or mashed potatoes (Arthur Lake).

DAUBE DE SERPENT PYTHON   DAUBE OF PYTHON

Cut four pounds of fillet from a young python. Dip it in flour mixed with salt, pepper and ginger. Whip a pound of butter with two quarts of cream. Add two glasses of sherry or a glass of any alcohol you please. Plunge the fillets in this sauce and let it simmer gently over low heat until the meat is cooked. Serve with corn or a green vegetable.

CIVET DE LION   CIVET OF LION

Singe and clean a lion's cub, preferably one six months old. Reserve a large casserole of blood to which you will add some vinegar. Cut the meat in pieces and add some unpeeled onions and some celery. Pour table wine over the mixture and let it stand at least twelve hours, stirring it every hour.

Pour off the liquid. Salt and pepper the meat. Place it in a better wine in which you put more aromatics with any spices you choose (do not forget to put in a little garlic). Let it cook until the grease rises. Skim. Continue the cooking until the meat is very tender. Then add the blood-vinegar mixture and remove from the fire. Serve with mushrooms and boiled onions.

Frédéric preparing his famed " canard au sang, " at the Tour d'Argent, about 1890

Seventeenth Course

A BAVARIAN CLERGYMAN WOULD HAVE THE FRENCH EAT MORE WISELY

With the débâcle over and the new Republic established, the French had only to plan for the future. Everything, in fact, incited them to it. Discoveries that were to revolutionize industry and daily life followed one after the other. French capitalism grew in power. Employees, workers were discontented. The bread they earned was worth its weight in labor. They formed syndicates, professional groups.

Cooks and chefs followed suit. Too numerous and poorly paid, they too formed a syndicate led by a man of vast experience: Thomas Génin (1).

Aided by Châtillon-Duplessis, author of books on cooking, Génin and his colleagues plunged into the struggle to re-appraise their profession. Thomas Génin was a little man, bubbling with energy. His colleagues called him the "Gambetta of the kitchen." When it came to rallying flagging courage, he had no equal. He organized meeting after meeting throughout France. In 1883 he began to preside weekly over a meeting of cooks to which—because of the patronage of Châtillon-Duplessis —experienced gastronomes and writers

---

(1) T. Génin died January 31, 1888, the victim of a "strange" accident on the Pont-des-Saints-Pères. Some thought that death might be the epilogue of a professional rivalry.

on gastronomy flocked. The meeting was held in a little room on the rue Lafitte. There statutes, inspired by a genuine love of the Art, were drawn up. Thomas Génin claimed that the discredit into which the profession of master-chefs had fallen was the result of the abuse that had been made of their uniform.

"This chef's cap," he declared, "this white jacket, which every little kitchen sub-assistant and every little pastry-cook wears on the street, has not retained in the public eye that sacer-dotal character befitting to the culinary profession."

Génin wanted to suppress the right to call oneself a "cook" unless one had obtained a certificate. According to him the right to wear the white jacket and chef's cap should be forbidden anyone who had not passed a certain number of examinations. But to reach that point, the profession would have to be reorganized from the bottom, professional schools opened, culinary competitions organized.

The first competition was held in December, 1883, on the rue Cadet, in the Grande Salle of the Grand Lodge of France. Many prominent persons mingled with the crowd of visitors. The contestants—all unknown to the general public—produced marvels in the way of set pieces, prepared dishes, unpublished recipes.

It was a great success and the experience encouraged the organizers to continue their efforts. For a good many years the "*Concours culinaire*," which was held regularly towards the end of March or the beginning of April, was one of the most Parisian spectacles. It moved first to the pavillon of the Ville de Paris, then to the Champs-Elysées. In 1889 we find it in one of the pavillons of the World's Fair; after that it was held in the Tuileries Gardens under an immense awning.

An innovation in 1908: to the culinary contest was added a "*Concours de cuisine régimentaire.*" The first *École de Cuisine Française* was to have less success. Opened in 1883, it closed its doors fifteen months later for lack of credit.

A KING OF THE EARTH : JULES GOUFFÉ

Thomas Génin did not benefit from the fame he deserved. His "corpora-tive"—or rather, "syndicalist"—activ-ities prejudiced people against him. In those days, the number one star of kitchen ranges and white caps was Jules Gouffé (1807-1877), the son of a Parisian pâtissier. Gouffé had been a pupil of Carême, and served under him in the kitchens of the Austrian Embassy in Paris.

WAITRESSES AT A " BOUILLON DUVAL "
(Photo Josse Lalance)

"Having embarked on a culinary career at an early age," he was to write, "I saw much, observed much, practiced much—in every sense of the word. I have had the opportunity of studying the works of our former *grands maîtres:* Loyer, the man who knew best how to serve a large piece of game; Léchard, the all-round expert, handling with superior talent every aspect of cuisine and Bernard, famed for the delicacy of his work. I was employed for seven consecutive years as cook and pastry cook by the illustrious Carême. The memory of those days has never made me unfair towards the present. I am not one of those who declare that French Cuisine is lost today and that it will never recover. Good things, true things, never die: they no doubt have their periods of decline, but sooner or later, with hard work, intelligence and good will, they recover."

After leaving Carême, Gouffé opened a restaurant on the rue Saint-Honoré. But he soon gave that up to head the kitchens of Napoléon III. In 1877, encouraged by Alexandre Dumas *père*, he took over the management of the kitchens at the Jockey Club.

Half a century after Gouffé's death, Paul Gauthier, then honorary president of the *Académie des Gastronomes*, sang his praises—with several reservations, however. He criticized Gouffé for having been the apostle of decorative cookery "which is the most detestable form of cuisine, such as that abominable mixture one is served in the Palaces proves.

"He thought of cooking only in terms of decoration. All his dishes were heavily laden with all sorts of ornaments, in plated ware or silver, piercing the meats which he topped with little rolls of vegetables, also too elaborate. Then the food was masked in a mosaic of sauces, white, yellow, red or green, in a sort of ceremonial robe... as if it were his duty to introduce it at Court."

Gauthier misunderstood the *Livre de Cuisine* which Gouffé published in the twilight of his life and which, for the past century, has been plagiarized by almost every writer of cookbooks. All of Gouffé's (1) professional integrity lies in a sentence from his preface: "I have never in my life written a recipe without constantly watching the clock and having the scales within reach."

Gouffé's great merit lay in the fact that he drew up strict rules for cooking. It was to Jules Gouffé that the songwriter, Charles Vincent dedicated his *Rois de la Terre* (Kings of the Earth).

A toi Gouffé cette chanson,
A toi dont le savoir extrême,
Élargit encore l'horizon
Découvert par Carême.

---

(1) Jules Gouffé had two brothers who were also chefs. The elder, Alphonse, was *officier de bouche* at the Court of St. James; Hippolyte was in charge of the kitchens of Count Schuvanoff, one of the finest *fin de siècle* epicures.

Gloire à vous Carême et Gouffé
Votre juste prépondérance
Dans tous les pays a greffé
Le renom glorieux de la France.

PAPUT-LEBEAU'S ADVICE

In 1883, a book was published —*Le Gastrophile*—by Paput-Lebeau, head chef at the hôtel of the *Cheval Blanc* (White Horse Hotel) in Angers. Unfortunately this volume is practically impossible to find today. But the advice Paput-Lebeau gave far and wide to those who wanted "food to nourish the body" deserves remembering.

"Always dine with cheerful people. The Ancients had fools and buffoons around the table to provoke laughter, the best of all aids for the digestion.

"Never go to the table when you are angry. Everything you eat will seem badly prepared and your digestion will be poor.

"Nor go to the table when you are over-heated by temper: wait until your blood has cooled.

"Never quarrel at the table. For example, a woman who chooses that moment to pick a quarrel with her husband and children, makes them bilious and predisposes herself to liver trouble.

"Exercise after eating disturbs the digestion. Many persons believe the contrary but they are mistaken, for the important function of digesting requires rest. You disturb it by moving about; you also disturb it by reading or by doing any work whatsoever.

"Look at the animals. As soon as they have eaten, they sleep and their instinct always directs them to do what is necessary for them. I do not say that like them we should sleep, but I advise imitating them by taking at least one hour of complete rest on leaving the table.

"Exercise is advisable before eating to rouse the appetite; but shun it, I repeat, when your stomach is full.

"Finish your meal by eating a little crust of bread. It helps digestion and cleans the teeth much better than any dentifrice your mouthwash may contain.

"Never eat anything you do not like. It is a mistake—under pretext of bringing up children well—to force them to eat everything, even things for which they have an instinctive aversion.

"If you are regular in your habits, take well-regulated meals and at stated hours. If you have a sickly or a delicate constitution, eat only when you are hungry. Eat slowly, masticate thoroughly; but to do that you will have to keep your teeth in very good condition.

"Drink slowly and not too often, especially at dinner."

SEBASTIAN KNEIPP'S GOOD FOOD

That was the era when hygienic advice and culinary recipes went hand in hand. At the same time as Paput-Lebeau, another prominent figure turned dietitian: Sebastian Kneipp (1821-1899).

"Frenchmen," he cried on every occasion, "you have created the finest cuisine in the world, but you abuse it... Your food is not healthy: your dishes are too highly seasoned, too spicy or too alcoholic. You are shortening your lives."

Sebastian Kneipp was not a cook, nor a doctor, nor even particularly an epicure: he was a clergyman, a native of Bavaria. He popularized throughout the world his method for curing ills and pains: hydrotherapy. Every day dozens of sick, of all nationalities, flowed towards the little Swiss village of Woerishofen where Kneipp held his consultations.

He had reached his sixties when he announced that he intended to reform French cuisine. Physically he was astonishingly vigorous, he declared, because of his habit of standing every morning under a cold shower for a quarter of an hour. A tall man, athletic in build, with long white hair that fell to his neck, he had strong features, black eyes, deepset and sparkling, and very heavy eyebrows. To everyone who came to him at Woerishofen, he recommended not only taking morning baths in icy water, but tight-fitting bathing suits and walking barefoot in the morning dew.

In 1888 a *Manuel de Cuisine Kneippiste* was published in France. In four years more than fifty thousand copies were sold. That was an unheard of success: in those days, a best seller seldom went beyond six or seven thousand copies.

"Of course," the author says, "I am not one of those esthetes who recommend eating nothing but boiled vegetables and fruits. As regards food, my rules are strict, but they are not discouraging. A rich diet, strengthening and, above all, simple, with very few spices, that is what one should have."

Within twenty years, France changed her alimentary regime and it is quite likely that Sebastian Kneipp's principles were partly responsible. At first it became the custom, at family meals, to cut down on the number of dishes. That was the first step towards the

DINER
DE LA
POULE AU POT

Donné
le
6
Février
1903

RESTAURANT
ROUGEMONT
dirigé
par
GABRIEL LÉVY

– MENU –
=

Potage Poule au Pot
Bisque d'Ecrevisses
Truite du Rhin Champerret
Caille à la Marie Stuart
Baron de Chézelle
Garniture Renaissance
Chapon du Mans à la Broche
Truffes braisées au Madère
Asperges Vertes sauce Hollandaise
Aspic de Foies Gras de Toulouse
Salade de Romaine
Nesselrode Glacée
Gâteau Mousseline
Desserts

VINS
Pauillac-Graves — Pomard 1885
Château-Giscours 1887 - Champagne
G.-H. Mumm Cordon Rouge
Curaçao Bols Blanc

tradition of the "one course dinner," almost universally adhered to today.

The vegetables Kneipp especially recommended were cabbage, followed by fennel and potatoes.

"As for potatoes," he said, "they are indispensable to mankind, especially to the poorer classes who, without them, would be hard put to it to be sure of their sustenance." While Kneipp did not take a definite stand against eating meat, he preferred farinaceous foods. "The simplest dishes are those in which only the basic farinaceous foods enter—and, above all, should not be seasoned with artificial ingredients. Those dishes are the most favorable to good health. Once you have become used to them, you give up meats without much effort."

Finally, in addition to cabbage, fennel, farinaceous foods and potatoes, a perfect Kneippist meal might also consist of "hart's-tongue fern soup" (or liver soup), "dandelion meatballs," "beer soup," "bilberry soup," or "horseradish broth."

FÉLIX FAURE
DEVOURS A LEG OF CAPON

Though the Kneipp theory had its followers, it had no effect on the *Grande Cuisine* of France and barely troubled the battalions of chefs, gastronomes, gourmets and guzzlers. Humorists lost no opportunity to poke fun at the "Cuire-assez" from Woerishofen(1) (as they called Kneipp).

From the more serious newspapers where state banquets were described in full detail, we learn that Jules Ferry(2) was one of the greatest trenchermen in Paris; that Jules Guesde(3) was a better orator when he spoke after a good meal; that Félix Faure(4) was especially fond of the leg of a capon *à la bourguignonne*.

"He grabs it from you," noted the celebrated Parisian reporter, Antoine de Restac, "raises it on a level with his eye, gazes at it benevolently until his eyes melt with tenderness. Then, without more ado, he devours it."

Charles Floquet(5) had a heartier appetite. He liked lobster salad and always took two helpings of duckling.

Casimir-Périer(6) detested beef *en daube*, but he made up for it on *ballottine* of pigeon (a cold meat dish).

"How can M. Clemenceau digest when he eats such quantities of *Galantine de Toulouse* so fast," asked Restac.

---

(1) A play on the words *cuirasser* (to protect as in armour) and *cuire-assez* (to cook enough).
(2) Jules Ferry, French statesman (1832-1893).
(3) Jules Guesde, politician, Marxist (1845-1922).
(4) Félix Faure (1841-1899), President of the Republic from 1895 to 1899.
(5) Charles Floquet (1828-1896), Président du Conseil in 1888.
(6) Casimir-Périer, Jean-Paul-Pierre (1847-1907), President of the Republic from June 27, 1894, to January 15, 1895.

CONTROVERSY OVER A MENU AT THE ÉLYSÉE

On October 8, 1896, to thank the Czar of Russia (Nicholas II) for having the happy idea of borrowing money from the thrifty French, the President of the Republic, Félix Faure, gave a dinner for him at the Élysée. Menu :

Birds' nest consommé; cream of chicken
Iced carp from la Creuse, sauce française
Saddle of fawn with pine seeds
Suprême of fowl with Périgord truffles
Terrine of lobster Toulousaine
Ortolans des Landes in tartlet shells
Oranges from Nice *gratinées*
Pheasants flanked with roast partridges
on *croustades*
Truffles *au champagne*
Foie gras *à la parisienne*
Francillon salad
Eggplant stuffed *à la fermière*
Artichoke hearts *à la créole*
Abricots and greengage plums from
Montmorency
Hazelnut ice
Waffles Condé
Dessert (sweets, cheese, fruit)

Wines:

Xérès *goutte d'or ;* Château-Lagrange *en carafe ;* Sauternes *en carafe ;* champagne rosé *en carafe ;* Château-Yquem 1876; Château-Lafitte 1875; Clos Vougeot 1874; Roederer *frappé*.

When French gastronomes studied that menu, they narrowed their lips resentfully. They could excuse the "Terrine of lobster Toulousaine" and the "Oranges *gratinées*," but to serve a foie gras at the beginning of the meal!... It was simply shocking! They said so frankly. They even wrote about it! That was the beginning of a long polemic which, growing more and more embittered, did not end until the chef of the President's kitchens was "removed."

On the other hand, a popular author was enchanted: Alexandre Dumas, the younger. At that famous dinner they had served Salade Francillon. Now, though Dumas had not created that recipe, he had popularized it in his latest play: *Francillon* (Act I, Scene 2).

Annette: Cook the potatoes in broth, cut them in slices as for an ordinary salad and, while they are still hot, season them with salt, pepper, a very good fruity olive oil, vinegar...

Henri: Tarragon?

Annette: Orléans is better; but that is not important. The important thing is half a glass of white wine: Château-Yquem, if possible. Plenty of *fines herbes* finely chopped. At the same time cook in court bouillon some very large mussels with a stalk of celery; drain carefully and add to the potatoes.

Henri: Not as many mussels as potatoes?

Annette: A third less. So that, little by little, you smell the mussels. You must not be able to detect it, neither must it be too strong. When the salad is made, toss it lightly: arrange in the shape of a *calotte de savant* (a wise man's skullcap) and cover it with sliced truffles.

Henri: Cooked in champagne?

Annette: Of course. This must all be done two hours before dinner so that the salad is very cold when served.

Henri: The salad bowl could be surrounded with ice.

Annette: No! No! No! You must not hurry it. It is very delicate and its various aromas must be allowed to blend quietly. Was the salad you ate today good?

Henri: Marvelous!

Annette: Well, follow my recipe, and you will have the same pleasure.

(Photo Josse Lalance)

RECIPES FOR "PLAIN" GOOSE LIVER FROM JULES GOUFFÉ

FOIE GRAS AU NATUREL   *GOOSE LIVER AU NATUREL*

Trim the liver, that is, remove the spleen and the adjacent parts as well as the blood vessels. Season it with salt, white pepper and spices. Sprinkle it with a dash of cognac. Let it steep in this seasoning for several hours.

Wipe it off and cook in goose fat, over a low heat, for forty-five minutes, to an hour according to the size of the liver.

Put the goose liver in an oval terrine. When it is almost cold, pour the fat from the cooking over it. When this fat is firmly set, cover it with a light layer of lard. Let it chill thoroughly.

Put the lid on the terrine. Tie a band of paper around the opening between the edge of the lid and the top of the pot. Keep in a dry, cool place.

FOIE GRAS BRAISÉ   *BRAISED GOOSE LIVER*

Season the liver and let it marinate in cognac. Wrap it in bards of very thin pork fat or with crépine of pork (pork caul).

Put it in a narrow casserole on a braising base with Madeira, Xérès or any other wine according to the nature of the preparation. Start it on the top of the stove, cover it and bake it in the oven forty-five minutes to one hour depending upon the size of the piece.

FOIE GRAS POCHÉ   *POACHED GOOSE LIVER*

The liver, seasoned as in the preceding recipes, is marinated in cognac. Poach it in butter, covered, for forty-five minutes to one hour according to the size.

FOIE GRAS EN CHAUSSON   *GOOSE LIVER TURNOVER*

Stud with truffles a large goose liver which you have selected for its firmness. Season it with salt, pepper and spices and let it marinate in a cool place for four hours. Seal it in butter on all sides and set aside to cool. Wrap it in dough shaped in the form of a turnover. Make an opening in the top of the turnover to let the steam escape. Decorate with bits of pastry and glaze. Bake in the oven forty-five minutes. When ready to serve, pour into the opening of the turnover several tablespoons of Sauce madère *which you have reduced, and add some truffles.*

Ce numéro est accompagné d'un supplément musical et de deux gravures en couleurs hors texte.

L'ILLUSTRATION

Prix du Numéro : 75 centimes.   SAMEDI 29 SEPTEMBRE 1900   58ᵉ Année — Nᵒ 3005

LE BANQUET DES MAIRES. — L'organisateur surveillant les préparatifs en automobile. — (Voir l'article, à la page 204.)

Eighteenth Course

THE MAYORS' BANQUET DOES NOT STOP PEOPLE FROM TALKING ABOUT CASSOULET

On September 22, 1900, towards eleven o'clock in the morning, 22,295 persons, full of their own importance and sporting top hats and black redingotes, met in the Tuileries Gardens. At the instigation of radical Ministers and leaders acting in the name of the Government, they had been invited to dine as guests of the Republic. Officially those leading magistrates of the town and county districts were there to be congratulated on their victory in the recent municipal elections and to make arrangements for their secret plan of what the powers behind the important "Toulouse Dispatch" called the "de-Christianization" of France.

This was the *Affaire des Congrégations*(1) (preparing for the separation of Church and State).

Those twenty-two thousand municipal magistrates would not know what it was all about till several weeks later. For the time being, they were all having a festive holiday under the autumn sun. Their prefects, their senators and deputies were present. To direct the guests and give them information the Prefecture of Police had mobilized all its men. M. Lépine himself superintended the maintenance of order.

By ten o'clock in the morning hun-

(1) Probably the Associations Law regulating terms relative to religious congregations.

dreds of curious spectators began to hurry towards the Tuileries. Shouts burst forth: "Hurrah for the Mayors! Hurrah for the Republic! Three cheers for Republican Algeria!"

There was a report that M. de Saint-Léger, Mayor of Limé (Aisne), who had recently sent an insulting letter to the Premier, M. Waldeck-Rousseau, had been refused admittance to the banquet hall. At the same time the Mayor of Limé learned that he had been removed from office that very morning.

A CANON SHOT MARKS A HISTORIC DATE

The guests stared in awed amazement at the splendor of the banquet hall which had been set up under an immense awning decorated with cockades and tricolor flags. It glittered with dazzling white linen, sparkling silver and the many-faceted reflections of crystal. Although there was no electricity, there was also no lack of light: according to the news-sheets, two hundred Denayrouse lamps (burning alcohol) shed "a lighting power of twenty thousand candles."

The guests sat down under the awning around nine immense tables. On each table: two rows of menus in the red and blue colors of the City of Paris, specially printed by the publisher Bauchet. Above their heads, long ribbons of different hues crisscrossed the room: with his invitation each guest had received the plan of the table at which he would be seated and an indication of the color he must follow to reach his place.

A canon roared, fired from the first floor of the Eiffel Tower. One minute later, M. Loubet, President of the Republic, accompanied by MM. Deschanel and Fallières, Presidents of the Senate and the Chamber respectively, entered and went to the dais. The guests rose in a body and applauded them. M. Loubet acknowledged the greeting with a wave of his hand and sat down. The guests resumed their seats and all eyes turned to the menus:

Hors d'œuvres; Fillet of beef *en Bellevue*, Duckling loaves from Rouen, Roast fowl from Bresse, Ballotine of pheasant Saint-Hubert; salade Potel; ices *succès Condé*; desserts.

Wines: Preignac and Saint Julien *en carafes*, Haut-Sauternes, Beaune, Morgon 1887, Champagne Montebello; Coffee, liqueurs.

That banquet of Mayors on September 22, 1900, marked a date in the history of French cuisine. Never before had such a vast number of guests been brought together at one meal. The honor of perfecting that "première" had been conferred upon the firm of Potel and Chabot. M. L'Hermite, the retired head of the firm, left his retreat in Coucy-le-Château, where he lived in the house that had once belonged to Gabrielle d'Estrées (favorite of Henri IV), to come to the aid of his successor, M. Legrand. The firm mobilized 1800 maîtres d'hôtels, 3,600 waiters and cooks, 300 dishwashers and 6 pages. They used 95,000 glasses, 60,000 forks and spoons, 250,000 plates and dishes, 8,000 tablecloths and 30,000 napkins.

As for provisions, they had bought about 5,000 pounds of fillets of meat, 5,000 pounds of pheasants, over 4,000 pounds of salmon, more than 5,000 pounds of duckling, about 1,300 quarts of mayonnaise, 5,000 pounds of fowl, 2,000 pounds of grapes, 10,000 peaches, 4,000 figs, 6,000 pears, 4,000 apples, 20,000 plums, 60,000 *petits fours...* They served 50,000 bottles of wine, 3,000 quarts of coffee, 1,000 quarts of liqueurs...

When, after M. Loubet's speech, the moment for toasts arrived, the doyen of the Mayors, M. Rigaud, exclaimed:

"Today is the happiest day of my life. For the first time I have the honor of approaching the Powers that be. Never would I have dreamed of being seated at the table of the Head of State and on the right hand of the Premier."

The choice of M. Rigaud to occupy that place of honor had caused a slight contretemps. If, at 82, he was "dean by right of age" he was not "dean by right of tenure." M. Adhémar Sautier, who claimed that title, had protested violently. To make amends, while dessert was being served, M. Loubet signed a decree conferring on M. Sautier the Legion of Honor.

TWENTY CASSOULETS... ONLY ONE SECRET

During this era controversies raged around a number of France's "national dishes": "pot-au-feu," "sauerkraut," "bouillabaisse," "tripes *à la mode de Caen.*" The most famous of these polemics was waged by the well-known gastronome, Edmond Richardin, over the recipe for "cassoulet"—a quarrel that is still not settled today. There is not a Frenchman alive who does not feel hunger gnawing at his vitals at the mere mention of that enchanting and glorious word "cassoulet." It is one of the standards of French bourgeois cooking. It is the "one dish" meal *par excellence*, the one that can be prepared, devoured, relished and enjoyed only at home.

On this point we are emphatic: the cassoulet is under no circumstances a restaurant dish. There are in existence some twenty recipes to which their

22,295 GUESTS !

creators have attached the name of *cassoulet*. Actually there are only three real cassoulets: the cassoulet of Castelnaudary, the cassoulet of Toulouse and, finally, the cassoulet of Carcassonne. In the controversies Richardin stirred up, the question was to establish exactly which one of the three was the leader.

The cassoulet is indisputably native to Castelnaudary. A certain Bringuier perfected the recipe, under rather indefinite circumstances. It is made with fresh pork, ham or pork knuckle, some sausage meat and fresh bacon rind. In Carcassonne, they add a shortened leg of mutton and, in the hunting season, a partridge. In Toulouse, in addition to these basic ingredients, they add some breast of pork, country sausage, mutton and especially preserved goose or duck (*confit d'oie ou de canard*). As for beans, they consider beans from Cazères and from Pamiers the best, not to mention the white beans from Alsace.

Balzac, Flaubert, Dumas the elder, even Anatole France have all sung the praises of cassoulet.

"I am going to lead you," says Anatole France in *Histoire comique*, "to a little tavern on the rue Vavin, chez Clémence, which makes only one dish, but what a superb dish it is! *Le cassoulet de Castelnaudary. Cassoulet de Castelnaudary* contains legs of preserved goose, beans previously blanched pork fat and little sausages. To be good, it must have cooked very slowly for a long time. Clémence's

cassoulet has been cooking for twenty years. She replenishes the pot sometimes with goose, sometimes with pork fat, sometimes she puts in a sausage or some haricot beans, but it is always the same cassoulet. The basis remains and this ancient and precious substance gives it the savor which one finds in the paintings of the old Venetian masters, in the amber flesh tints of their women. Come, I want you to taste Clémence's cassoulet."

Monsieur France had been misled, it seems: the cassoulet to which Clémence adds preserved goose is not that of Castelnaudary but of Toulouse.

That "cassoulet quarrel" was started by an article signed by the Parisian columnist, Antoine de Restac, in which he praised the Castelnaudary recipe. What a row that kicked up! Forty-eight hours later, his colleague, Emmanuel Tivollier—the poet of "Duck Pâté"—replied sharply by publishing in *Le Figaro* a recipe for making that "food for the gods," the "Cassoulet Royal from the City of Carcassonne."

Then followed a deluge of letters from Paris and from every corner of the provinces, congratulating Restac, admonishing Tollivier. There was talk of a "cassoulet briard," a "cassoulet des mers" made with fish as a base, a "cassoulet bourguignon," a "cassoulet alsacien"...

Fulbert-Dumonteil (1830-1909) was also heard from. This man from Périgord was one of the most brilliant writers on gastronomy at the beginning of the twentieth century. The literary salons were inclined to poke fun at him and even the very austere *Revue des Deux Mondes* ridiculed his grandiloquent flights in praise of truffles from his native province or the "delights of sole."

"Jean-Camille!" exclaimed Restac, "Why, he could even make poetry out of a codfish." At the time, Jean-Camille Fulbert-Dumonteil furiously defended his recipe for "cassoulet *à la périgordine*." Important personalities in arts and letters and the world of politics joined in the controversy, among them, benevolent "little father" Fallières, again President of the Chamber and future President of the Republic: he summoned half a dozen writers on gastronomy to his house at Loupillon. There, in the presence of his delighted guests, he concocted a "cassoulet of my own recipe" which, they assure us, was worth its weight... in beans.

But before I give you a few recipes, I must emphasize an important detail about which most culinary works are silent: the secret of the seven skins!

When the cassoulet is put in a very slow oven, a coating or film slowly forms at the top of the glazed earthenware casserole in which it must be cooked. Once this sort of "skin" is formed, you must break it by stirring it gently into the rest of the contents. Then put the casserole back in the oven until a second skin forms, like the first, and just as delectable. Break the second skin: stir it into the contents of the dish as before. And continue that operation until the seventh skin has formed and has been stirred into the cassoulet. If you neglect to break the seven skins, you cannot have a perfect cassoulet, whether Castelnaudary, Toulouse or Carcassonne.

A FEW GENUINE CASSOULET RECIPES

CASSOULET DE CASTELNAUDARY

Set a quart of white shell beans, which have been soaked for several hours in water, to cook with 2/3 of a pound of breast of pork, about a cup of fresh bacon rind tied in a bunch, a carrot, an onion stuck with cloves, a bouquet garni *and three cloves of garlic. Salt the beans lightly and cover them well with water. Cook until you have a very weak broth.*

Meanwhile brown some pork fat or even better some goose fat, about 1 pound, 8 ounces of pork chine, 1 pound of boned loin of mutton; salt and pepper. When the meats

209

are well browned, put in the earthenware pot in which they have cooked a scant half-pound of chopped onions, a bouquet garni and two cloves of garlic. Cover and cook, moistening from time to time with some good broth. Add several tablespoons of good tomato purée.

When the beans are almost done, take out the vegetables, which you will use as a garnish, and the bouquet garni. Put the meat back in the pot, add a garlic sausage and a piece of homemade sausage. Let it simmer gently for an hour. Strain all the meats that are in the beans and slice them (removing the skin from the large sausage).

Sprinkle with a layer of coarse breadcrumbs; moisten with goose fat. Let it cook gently in the oven for an hour and a half... but do not forget to break the skin seven times (*Prosper Montagné, born in Castelnaudary*).

LE CASSOULET ROYAL DE LA CITÉ DE CARCASSONNE

The formula is the same as in the preceding recipe, but to it is added a shortened leg of mutton which has been boned, studded with garlic, and three-quarters braised in advance. Also added are a couple of partridges half-cooked and cut in pieces.

"Given the quantity of meat used for this truly royal cassoulet," Tivollier suggests, "it is to our interest to increase the quantity of beans. We must also use a larger earthenware pot to accommodate all the contents."

This method is of prime importance in preparing a cassoulet. "Originally," explains Richardin, "the superiority of the people from Castelnaudary in the art of making this glorious dish successfully, stemmed solely from the fact that all good bourgeois houses had a wood-burning oven, a baker's oven, and that it was heated 'discreetly,' to avoid drying it out, with piny furze from the mountains." In the same way Tivollier suggests that the use of dried brambles is to be highly recommended. But unfortunately there are few people nowadays who still have a wood-burning stove at their disposal.

LE CASSOULET DE TOULOUSE

The recipe is the same as that for Castelnaudary. But you add confit d'oie (preserved goose), a Toulouse sausage, some fairly lean pieces of mutton, a pig's foot *three-quarters cooked. You will find* confit d'oie *in a good pork butcher's shop. But you will do better to prepare it yourself; it will keep for several months. The recipe:*

Take the meatiest pieces of fowl and let them soak 24 hours in salt; then plunge them in a pot containing some melted goose fat and let them simmer for three or four hours. Finally arrange them in stone jars and cover them completely with hot fat.

CASSOULET A LA PÉRIGORDINE
CALLED "CASSOULET FULBERT-DUMONTEIL"

1. *Blanch about a quart and a half of choice haricot beans, white as snow and dry as matches. Drain them, put them in fresh water and cook till half done.*

2. *Meanwhile place some tender and succulent pieces of lamb in a large kitchen casserole; it is essential to add a wing and two legs of* confit d'oie *(preserved goose)* à la Toulousaine, *not forgetting a duck's neck stuffed with artistically minced sausage meat and truffles from the Périgord. Moisten your appetizing (sic) legs and your truffled neck (sic) with six tablespoons of good goose fat, unctuous, odoriferous and amber-color. In ten minutes wing, legs, and mutton will take on a beautiful golden color. Add a fine sausage and cover with the well-drained beans.*

3. *Without losing a minute, brown some onions and cloves of garlic chopped quite fine and mixed with a bit of chopped bacon.*

4. *All that remains to be done is to moisten this mixture with three big cups of bouillon and five spoons of tomato sauce.*

5. *After reducing it to the proper amount (by patient and gentle cooking), sprinkle your dish with breadcrumbs mixed with parsley. Brown to a beautiful color and serve in the large casserole.*

What a fine cassoulet that is! "It is better than a rose," the good Fulbert assures us: "The flower dies, the dish remains and its perfume equals the perfume of the flowers" (sic).

LE CASSOULET BRIARD   CASSOULET OF THE BRIE REGION

This is the same basic recipe as for cassoulet de Castelnaudary, *but you add half a hare cut in pieces and a partridge or a pheasant, also cut up.*

Nineteenth Course

LÉON DAUDET, EXPERIENCED GASTRONOME, ORGANIZES THE FIRST GONCOURT LUNCHEON

Ten men of letters met at lunch in one of the state dining rooms of the Grand Hôtel on February 26, 1903. They were the ten charter members of the Académie Goncourt: Léon Daudet, Huysmans, Octave Mirbeau, the two Rosny, L. Hennique, Paul Marguerite, Gustave Geffroy, Elémir Bourges, Lucien Descaves. In accordance with the will of Edmond de Goncourt, they were to meet once a month at lunch to draw up final regulations for their Assembly and, especially, to allot the award to the author of "the best imaginative book in prose of the year."

That day Octave Mirbeau was in a bad mood. He did not hesitate to let his comrades know that he was not at all satisfied with the choice of the Grand Hôtel as a meeting place. The restaurant was too pompous and he was afraid of getting a stomach ache.

Mirbeau was mainly annoyed with Léon Daudet whom he accused of having forced this meeting place on them. Daudet ignored him: he was already absorbed in the pleasures of the table. A passionate gastronome, this political companion of Maurras was never loath to recall his finest memories of food. He told the story of a dish he had invented when he was a medical student and frequented the pension Laveur:

"It was a filling dish, but tasty and was made as follows: one layer of white haricot beans, one layer of fried potatoes and on top of that, two fried eggs." Léon Daudet had baptized this mixture *kaulback* ("in memory of I don't know which Russian general").

Mathilde, the waitress, exclaimed as she watched Daudet and his companions heaping their plates full: "I wonder how you can all swallow such dog-food!"

His comrades at medical school at that time were the brothers Babinsky; one of them was to become a famous neurologist; the other was to publish, under the name of Ali Bab, a culinary "outline" that is still authoritative today.

"One day," Daudet relates, "I had a violent argument with them as to whether chicory salad lightly sprayed with absinthe should or should not be served with foie gras. I was against it, for in my opinion the taste of oil kills the foie gras."

Later, Daudet was to use his pen secretly in the service of cooking—and of his second wife, his cousin, Marthe Allard. With her husband's help, Marthe has left us several cook books published under the pseudonym of Pampille, among them *Les Bons Plats de France* and especially *Les Almanachs gourmands de L'Action Française.*

If Léon Daudet had influenced his colleagues' choice towards the Grand Hôtel at that first luncheon of the Académie Goncourt, it was because the

LÉON DAUDET *(Photo Harlingue)*

chef in that hotel was Auguste Escoffier (1847-1938), one of the greatest cooks of the age. But despite Auguste Escoffier, the ten Goncourt academicians soon agreed with Mirbeau—the Grand Hôtel was too pompous and dignified. They left it for the *Restaurant Champeau*, place de la Bourse: but soon—too crowded this time—they moved to the *Café de Paris*, which sheltered them until war was declared in 1914. Then they discovered Drouant, place Gaillon, who was to owe his fame to them.

THE CRUEL FATE OF A FUTURIST COOK

A vast number of French cooks met their death beside their field kitchens on the battlefields during World War I. Among them: Jules Maincave. Few, even among the erudites in the culinary art, remember the big friendly fellow with the soft, dreamy eyes. And yet he began to be famous in 1914. Raoul Ponchon devoted a whole gazette in verse to him and many were the persons of mark in Parisian society who dined at the restaurant on the Left Bank where Maincave was in charge of the ovens. There a dadaist cuisine was created and served by a futurist chef. It was not so absurd as

it seems. But let Maincave speak for himself:

"The French art of cooking hovers deplorably around a dozen recipes; the same dishes appear on tables, christened and re-christened a hundred times with amazing names to hide their mediocre sameness. For three centuries there have been no really new dishes in France.

"First of all I denounce the two Bastilles of modern cuisine: mixtures and aromatics. Tradition excludes some of them and authorizes many others. For example: oil mixed with vinegar forms a classic sauce but the thought of mixing rum and pork juice is considered heteredox. Why?

"As for seasonings, they are pitiably limited. We are still using bayleaf, thyme, parsley, scallions... whereas the progress of modern chemistry would enable us to use roses, lilacs, lilies of the valley, just as well.

"There is nothing more delicious, in my opinion, than a beef with *kummel*, garnished with rounds of bananas stuffed with Gruyère cheese; or a purée of sardines in Camembert; a whipped cream *à la tomate* sprinkled with brandy or a chicken with lilies of the valley."

Those words came as a shock to the average Frenchman to whom, except for *daubes* simmered *à point*, creamed dishes, chicken *à la périgordine* or simple *meunière* cooking (lightly floured and fried in butter), there was no cooking worthy of the name. But no

one who has travelled can forget fish from the Black Sea with essence of rose, or marrow stuffed with yogurt from Jordan, brochettes of meat with coconut milk from Indonesia, or even young monkey stuffed with peanuts—a favorite dish on the shores of the Niger. All that is as good as a venison from Alsace accompanied by barquettes (oval-shaped tartlet shells) filled with gooseberry jelly.

It is a pity Maincave died too soon!

He met nothing but mockery and ridicule from the defenders of our traditions. He was, perhaps, a forerunner.

I am writing these lines from a sixth-floor room facing on a court. It is Sunday: the weather is beautiful; all the windows are open wide. I look down into a half a dozen kitchens where as many meals are being prepared. And what do I see? Two, three, four and five chickens ready to be

roasted. One only—the one that will be served on the table of the colonel on the third floor to the right—seems to have been stuffed. And yet the Marquis de Cussy has listed 92 ways of cooking chicken!

At this point I begin to have my doubts! Granted, if Maincave were still alive and had succeeded in putting over certain of his creations, would I see in my neighbors' kitchens today anything but the classic Sunday roast chicken?

But to go back to our futuristic chef and his adventures. On the third day of the mobilization in 1914, Maincave found himself in the 90th Infantry regiment. Appointed company cook, he threw away the pamphlets on cooking the Army handed him. On mature reflection he concocted a mixture of herbs which he had gathered around the trenches and decorated his cooking with them. With these aromatics he seasoned his two specialties:

Bifteck d'attaque (Beefsteak *d'attaque*) and Purée of cheese *au pinard* (with wine) which was the special delight of his fellow soldiers. The fame of Maincave as a cook soon spread beyond his unit. It reached the general staff of Gouraud who, intrigued, one day went to eat Maincave's famous stew.

When he had finished the first dish, the officer wiped his moustache with the back of his hand and sent for the cook:

"It is excellent," he said, "I'll have some more."

"Colonel!" exclaimed Maincave, "What you have just told me gives me more pleasure than if I had been granted the cross!"

"You shall have that too," replied Gouraud.

And, in fact, he did—a very pretty wooden cross that was planted over his stomach a few days later in the midst of the battle of the Somme. A shell had blown him up along with his field-kitchen.

"Maincave," his lieutenant had just told him, "take shelter."

"You can't cook in a cave," the cook had replied. "No German pots are going to make me leave mine."

Those were his last words.

(Photo Harlingue)

ONE OF JULES MAINCAVE'S RECIPES

FILLET OF SOLE A LA CRÈME CHANTILLY
FILET DE SOLE A LA CRÈME CHANTILLY

Cut out the fillets from some nice soles. Keep the head and bones. Marinate the fillets in rum and put a match to them. Pound the head and bones to powder and sprinkle it over the fish. Brown the fish and surround them with a mousse of Chantilly cream to which you have added a little purée of tomatoes. Serve the fillets very hot and the cream ice-cold. Pour over your fillets, in driblets, six drops of an extract of any perfume you choose.

... AND OTHER MORE CLASSIC RECIPES

CARBONADE DE VEAU   CARBONADE OF VEAL

For four or five people, take a 3 pound fillet of veal and cut it in half lengthwise. Prepare a stuffing with 1 1/3 cups of bread crumbs, about a cup of freshly chopped breast of veal, 2 eggs, salt and pepper. Place this stuffing between the two pieces of fillet and tie securely. Dust with flour and brown in butter. Add a little broth to the pan and cook for two hours over low heat. At the end of the first hour, toss into the sauce 20 little onions which you will have sautéed until they are golden brown.

FRICASSÉE DE POULET   CHICKEN FRICASSEE

Cut a chicken in pieces. Cook it about forty minutes in a mixture of white wine and water, with salt, pepper, garlic, a bouquet garni, *an onion, a carrot and some bacon (it will not be served with the chicken).*

Make a white roux with butter, flour and the broth (from the cooking) to which you return the pieces of chicken, and add some mushrooms and—why not?—a few truffles.

When ready to serve add a thickening made by combining egg yolks, cream and the juice of a lemon. Serve surrounded with fried croutons.

THE END OF A GOOD DINNER, AT THE TWILIGHT OF " LA BELLE ÉPOQUE "

(Photo Josse Lalance)

Twentieth Course

AFTER
THE 1918 ARMISTICE
FRENCH CUISINE
TURNS DEMOCRATIC

"The door opens. We enter and straight ahead of us we see an imposing stove and behind it a chef, more majestic than a president, in a huge velvet cap—Prosper Montagné. Clad in white, with spectacles astride his nose, he is as red and shining as his most beautiful casseroles. He looks exactly as his fame would lead us to expect.

"What a handsome chef! What a fine-looking man, attentive, accurate and masterly. We are spellbound. We allow him to take our cane and our hat. You should see how our Prosper devotes his undivided attention to a sauce such as Guillaume Vinot never could have made: he is a scholar dedicated to Science, a true mandarin of Good Food. In addressing him one is tempted to use the one word the dignity of his office demands: Maître..."

This portrait of the most famous chef of the last fifty years is drawn by Henri Béraud. To perpetuate the memory of Prosper Montagné, his name was given to the Goncourt of gastronomy, the *grand prix* of the finest cooks in France.

Montagné has left us a number of cook books: *Les Délices de la Table*, a little treatise on transcendent cooking for the use of persons with good taste; *Le Manuel du Bon Cuistot*, a collection of recipes published in the *Bulletin des*

Armées; Le Grand Livre de Cuisine, with a preface by Béraud. He collaborated on a *Dictionnaire de la Table* with Escoffier and with Dr. Gottschalk, an eminent gastronome and collector of ancient and modern kitchen utensils.

After World War I, Prosper Montagné's restaurant, rue de l'Échelle, remained for more than ten years the place in France where one ate the best food. It was also the most expensive. Nevertheless Parisian society stood in line at the door to wait for a table. France was then going through its "wild years;" it was the day of the new millionaires and the last Russian princes. In one evening, the Prince of Wales, escorting Jeanne Marnac, gave up his table to André Citroën whose name was soon to be blazoned in letters of fire from the top of the Eiffel Tower; and at the next table, Maurice Chevalier, in the company of Yvonne Vallé, pretended not to see Fréhel, the great realistic singer, although he owed her much.

FOR BRILLAT-SAVARIN, A PIOUS THOUGHT AND A BANQUET

On February 6, 1926, Paris celebrated the centenary of Brillat-Savarin. Naturally Montagné was entrusted with directing the banquet given in the *grande salle des maréchaux* at the Hôtel Crillon. The ceremony on the threshold of the house in which Brillat-Savarin died—at the corner of the rue des Filles-Saint-Thomas—was quickly expedited. The guests were in a hurry to sit down at the table... menus had already been secretly circulated.

Hors d'œuvres: Rissoles of foie gras *du Bugay*; smoked sausage from Valromey; and a few other little appetizers, all washed down with a *Chablis*. Steamed anchovies with crawfish sauce (the way Mme Briguet made them for the dinner of the *Confrérie du curé de Talissiaud*). Gourmets have a choice between Chablis and Château-Cheval-blanc, 1914.

Truffled turkey *Baron Richerand*, accompanied by sausages. To drink: *Grande réserve Bouchard aîné et fils*, 1911 (*Côte de Nuits*).

Salade de l'émigré, according to a manuscript and apocryphal note left by M. Albrignac.

Cheeses: (Here a debate will be opened on the Fourteenth Aphorism, but they will be nonetheless accompanied by the *Réserve Bouchard aîné et fils*, 1911).

Pyramid of vanilla and rose meringue glacée with Heidsieck Dry Monopole (en magnum) and Pol-Roger (en magnum).

Fruits from the Ile-de-France; Coffee *à la Du Belloy*; *vieille eau-de-vie de cognac et la liqueur des Belles.*

HE COOKS MUTTON
THE WAY CARÊME DID

Montagné swore by Carême only. He came into possession of Antonin's manuscript—notes that were found in Talleyrand's archives—which were often an inspiration to him, particularly when a group of sheep-raisers asked him to arrange a dinner, for propaganda purposes, composed solely of dishes made from mutton. The banquet was held, not in the rue de l'Echelle, but at a former comrade's of Prosper Montagné, *au Picardy*, in the Batignolles quarter.

"Well, Monsieur Montagné," one of the guests said that evening, "have you managed to produce miracles?"

"Miracles?... No!" replied the celebrated chef, "simply good food."

He gave them fried sheep's trotters *à la Rouennaise;* Pascaline of lamb; Navarin or Alycot of mutton (a ragoût) with apples and turnips. Bottom round of young mutton roasted; sugared *tourte* of mutton *à la Limousine*.

M. Arbelot, one of the guests, later published the recipe for Pascaline of lamb as Montagné prepared it that day. *Pascaline d'agneau:* Take 4 lambs' heads (they must be perfectly scalded); clean and soak them, along with the 4 brains and the 4 tongues. For your forcemeat, sauté 3 lambs' livers with fresh bacon, *fines herbes*, salt, pepper, onions, and 12 lambs' feet cooked with the tongues. Cook the brains separate-ly. When the tongues and the brains are cooked, dice them, add mushrooms and shape them into 12 croquettes.

Now take 4 blanched heads of lamb and fill them with the forcemeat; sew them up securely. On top of them place several slices of lemon and cook in a good casserole.

Have a dozen larded lambs' sweet-breads ready; keep the throats dry; prepare a smooth sauce into which you have put 2 handfuls of mushrooms, reduce it and bind with 6 egg yolks. Then take the heads out of the casse-role, drain, remove thread, arrange on a long dish, nose facing out; cut each foot in two and put 3 of those between each head; pour the sauce over them and add the 12 fried croquettes, 12 larded lambs' sweetbreads and 12 croutons of bread cut to look like cocks' combs (fried in butter); toss the lambs' throats with the mushrooms into the sauce and cover the heads with it.

Though Montagné was the leading caterer of France, he was unfortunately a deplorable business man. Little by little his affairs worsened until, in the end, he was obliged to cut and run. Soon, in place of the luxurious restau-rant with its purple banquettes, there was only a café-bar, a sort of quick-lunch counter for people in a hurry, midinettes and sales clerks. That was, indeed, the "revenge of lemonade over Chambertin!"

Camille Labroue, a strange person, both journalist and restauranteur-poet,

BERNARD ZIMMER,   PAUL FUCHS,   M. DEKOBRA,   A. WARNOD,   R. KERDYK,   A. DE SEGONZAC,   MAC ORLAN,   H.
CLAUDE BLANCHARD,   R. LEFEBVRE

wrote four definitive lines explaining the reason for Montagné's failure:

On picole aujourd'hui et sable la chopine
Où l'univers gourmand était habitué
Car le grand Montagné dut fermer sa propine
Il paya trop le fisc : c'est le fisc qui l'a tué!

(Today they drink out of half-litre mugs where once the world of gourmets was at home, for the great Montagné has been obliged to close his doors. The heavy taxes he had to pay have ruined him.)

Taxes, perhaps, but also the wild extravagances into which innumerable parasitic friends dragged him were the cause of Montagné's downfall.

On the eve of World War II, Parisians saw on the Boulevard Saint-Marcel an old gentleman of fine bearing, but walking with difficulty, trudging every evening towards a little restaurant with fixed prices: *Chez Rat*, an eating place for taxi drivers and lonely bachelors. The old gentleman was the former "greatest caterer in France." He went there to dine on a simple plate of soup.

224

THE FAMOUS "EVENINGS" OF THE "CRAPOUILLOT"

The stews in army camps, the trench "kitchens," the fourth of wine with bromide added, had given the soldiers of 1914-1918 such a longing for wholesome food, that once back home again, they devoted themselves to making up for the good food they had missed.

Those were also the "wild years" for any bistro in the quarter whose owner hailed from Cantal, Aveyron, Périgord, or Béarn, with his batch of recipes from "back home." Gastronomic societies, the *Confréries de gueule*, groups of devotees of good food, had never been as numerous as in that era which came to an end in 1940. Doctors and lawyers were among the first to join the gourmet groups: they were soon followed by Parisian stock brokers, tennis players, city officials, police commissioners, porters, shirtsleeve piano players, manufacturers, café waiters, magicians and prestidigitators, employees of the pari mutuel betting office.

225

Soon syndicates and various party groups were involved in those feasts that were intended to be fraternal only: dinners given by certain professions even attained the importance of political banquets.

Several of those "brotherhoods of the table" became famous. Among others, the famous "*Dîners du Crapouillot*," which for ten years brought together periodically artists and men of letters at the *Petit Véfour*, the *Petite Chaise, Au Clairon des Chasseurs à pied* and finally *chez Dagorno*, around Jean Galtier-Boissière, the Rabelaisian director of the revue called "*Le Crapouillot*." Often those evenings ended in epic and comical expeditions.

One night, twenty some "crapouillots"—many of whom are today weighed down with academic honors— wearing top hats, rushed in columns of four from the porte de Pantin to the Faubourg Saint-Honoré, singing the refrains of Montéhus, swooping down in a wild charge on the Presidency of the Republic. Another evening Francis Carco led the whole table to a shady night-club in Montmartre and pushed François Mauriac into the best seat, while men, imitating women, painted and dressed as dancers, performed on the stage and then moved from table to table.

In the early morning hours, Paul Reboux took down the confidences of several "good earners," in a brothel in the Chapelle quarter where the group had once again been led by Carco.

GALTIER-BOISSIÈRE, *by Oberlé*

A FEW RECIPES FOR DINNERS FOR FRIENDS

CIVET DE LIÈVRE ARISTIDE BRIAND
CIVET OF HARE ARISTIDE BRIAND

This recipe was actually invented by the famous statesman.
Cut your hare in regular pieces and brown them in butter. When they are nicely browned, add 12 little pieces of pork fat and 3 medium onions. Mix well; toss in 2 spoons of flour and stir a long time. Add 5 crushed garlic cloves. In the sauté-pan pour some red Macon wine and beef broth until the meat is completely covered. Season with thyme, bayleaf, 12 shallots and a bouquet of parsley. Cook for 3 hours on low heat.

Remove the pieces of hare. Put them in a deep terrine with pork fat, 24 fine mushrooms, 6 more cloves of garlic and 24 minced shallots. Pour the sauce over it. Finish cooking your hare in the oven where you will leave it for six hours.

CANARD EN CIVET   DUCK STEW

Cut up a duck and brown it in 1/4 of a pound of pork fat cut in pieces and a little butter. When it is well browned, remove the pieces and replace them with 3 or 4 onions which you will cook till they turn golden, but not brown. Add a little flour and let it brown. Then return duck and pork to the casserole. Pour over them some champagne and set it ablaze.

Moisten with 2 glasses of Burgundy and a little broth. Add a bouquet garni, some appropriate spices, salt and pepper. Cook over a low heat for an hour and a half. Skim the sauce and strain it. Add 1/4 lb. of mushrooms and cook 15 minutes more.

CURNONSKY
WATCHING OVER A SAUCE
(*Photo Keystone*)

Twenty-first Course

CURNONSKY, GRAND SEIGNEUR AND PRINCE

On July 22, 1956, about ten o'clock in the morning, a few pedestrians were walking along the Square Laborde, near the Saint-Augustin Church, when suddenly there was a great shout—a man, falling from a third floor window, hit a veranda and crashed on the pavement! Men and women rushed towards the limp, disjointed body, lying outstretched on its back. Some one took the head between his hands, not knowing exactly what else to do. The eyes half opened, stared at the sky a second, then became fixed in death.

The man who had just breathed his last was the prince of gastronomes: Maurice-Edmond Sailland, known as Curnonsky. He was in his ninety-fourth year.

A throng of curiosity-seekers gathered around the corpse of what had been one of the most popular figures in Paris. Mme. Beaufils, the concierge of the building where the man had lived for nearly half a century, pushed her way through the crowd. Over her arm she carried a pillow and a cover. Already the siren of a police ambulance could be heard in the distance. A doctor—a neighbor, Dr. Jegou—leaned over the body.

"Nothing more to be done here," he said. "The vertebral column is broken in several places. He has literally broken his back."

229

THE CHAUD-FROID
KILLED ITS
GRANDFATHER

Among all those whose names are still connected with the history of French cuisine, Curnonsky is the only one who lived exclusively from gastronomy. He could have made a fortune if he had consented to lend his name to publicity slogans. But he always refused. Prince of fantasies, in his heart Curnonsky was fundamentally a grand seigneur.

A famous brand of liqueur offered him millions on the sole condition that he allow "Cur's Old Cure" to appear on the label of each bottle. He refused. When some manufacturers of margarine offered him an income for life if he would consent to admit publicly that margarine could replace butter, he replied simply:

"Nothing takes the place of butter."

He accepted only one annuity, the one the Métro offered in the form of free transportation.

"That is very nice," said Cur, "but they owe it to me. There are never any victims of accidents on the subway. Now that they have one, it's only natural for them to do something about it."

(In 1930 Curnonsky had slipped on a dirty station platform. He cracked his pelvis and was obliged to remain in the Cochin Hospital three months for treatment. When he came out he received twenty thousand francs indemnity and a lifetime pass on the Métro.)

Cur was born in Angers, October 28, 1862. His mother died in giving birth to him and the next day his father disappeared forever. He was brought up by his grandmother. As it happens, the future prince had a real title to nobility. His great grandmother, the blessed Jeanne Sailland, had been beatified. "A special rescript" of the Vatican exempted Jeanne's descendants and their guests from abstaining from meat on Fridays.

When he was twelve, Maurice Sailland "went up" to Paris to prepare for the *Normale Supérieure* (training college for the professorate), but he soon gave that up to plunge into journalism. At the time of the Franco-Russian Entente he used, for the first time, the pseudonym he was to make famous: he sent an open letter, addressed to the *Journal* and signed Curnonsky, to Émile Zola who had just suffered a second rebuff from the Académie Française. The letter was published. A few days later, Sailland received a money order drawn to the name of Curnonsky with a letter from the editor-in-chief asking him for more articles.

"That day," Cur was to say in later years, "I buried Maurice Sailland."

That rather ridiculous pseudonym caused him several unfortunate experiences. In 1914, on the Island of Bréhat, for example, he was arrested and held in prison several days as "a Russian spy in the pay of the Bulgarians."

HE HAD NO DINING ROOM IN WHICH TO RECEIVE HIS FRIENDS

From the time he entered literary and journalistic circles, Cur was obsessed with a passion for good food. He had, it is true, a certain predisposition to it: he was six feet one inch tall and weighed 264 pounds. Moreover he had such a hearty appetite that two invitations to dinner for the same evening did not daunt him.

He was charming when the hors d'œuvres were served, suave during the fish course, in high spirits during the "main course," truculent as soon as the cheeses appeared and just a little bawdy from then on. Hostesses vied with one another for the honor of inviting him to dinner.

A series of brochures on regional cooking and the best food in France made his name a byword to all lovers of good food throughout the nation. So well known was he, in fact, that in 1927 when, on the initiative of *Paris-Soir*,

five thousand gastronomes, famous cooks and celebrated restaurant owners were invited to elect a prince, Curnonsky was the man they chose. After that honors and invitations followed in quick succession. There was no dinner or banquet of distinction in France at which the organizers did not urgently request the presence of the prince.

"To fulfill my functions correctly," he wrote to one of his old friends, "I ought to have twelve mouths."

Aside from the diners that sometimes bored him—he made a great effort never to show it—Curnonsky led a very simple life in his modest apartment on the Square Laborde.

"Look," he would remark ironically, "the votes of my kind electors have crowned a poor man of letters, an unpretentious, easy-going man who, since reaching his majority, has had neither chef, nor first-rate cook, nor kitchen, nor wine cellar, nor dining room; who has always been satisfied with little and has never known the joy of receiving his friends in his own home."

As long as he lived, Cur never used the telephone. He preferred the newspaper to the radio, the theater to the cinema. He read voraciously anything that came to hand, no matter what. But if an author made the slightest error in any matter connected with the art of good food, he fumed with rage.

"Flaubert a gastronome! Come now! Don't make me laugh! How could he have written in *L'Éducation sentimentale*" (here Cur quotes from memory): "The bottles of wine were warming on the stove, the knife-blades glistened beside the oysters... the table practically disappeared under the mass of game and fruits..."

"It's outrageous! Game was served before the hors d'œuvres, wines warmed on the stove and oysters eaten with a knife! Not to mention his questionable references to 'Turban of rabbit *a la Richelieu*' and a certain 'Potted head of sturgeon'...?"

HIS BEST VENTURE: THE ACADEMY OF GASTRONOMES

One year after he was elected, *Sa Rondeur Cur I*—who had already been obliged to accept the presidency of some hundred societies—decided to organize an official group of connoisseurs. He therefore created the Academy of Gastronomes, taking his inspiration directly from the statutes of the Académie Française. Each member-elect must eulogize a sponsor chosen from among the "Great Gastronomes of History."

The choice of forty members proved to be a delicate matter. He had to take care not to offend anyone, but also to keep out all those clever publicity agents of gastronomy who—under cover of some vague brotherhood or of newspaper articles—prostituted the art of Good Food.

And right here it would seem fitting for me to recall the names of the charter members: Curnonsky, André Robine, Fernand Fleuret, Desombiaux, Édouard de Pomiane, Baron d'Aiguy, Léon Abric, Raymond Brunet, Maurice Brillant, Chambre, Charbonnel, Baron de Douvres, Gaston Derys, Simon Arbellot, Gaston Gérard, Rousset, Jobert, Marc Varennes, Maeterlinck, Paul Megnin, Paul Beinex, Paul Reboux, La Brusse, Chauvelot, Chaix, Gabion, Marquis de Polignac, Gaston Thierry, Laurens Frings, Fernand Payen, Millaud, Duplan, Paul Gaultier, Asselin, Justin Godart, Maringer, Malachouski, Tardieu, Robert Burnand.

Raymond Brunet had already published more than fifty volumes in praise of wine and several lists of gastronomes. Paul Reboux had produced two or three witty collections of original recipes; and Robert Burnand, a *Guide des Gourmands de Paris*. André Robine was president of the *Club des Purs-cent*. Paul Megnin was the author of several books on hunting and on gastronomy.

A FORTUNE
AT RIEC-SUR-BELON

As the prince refused to exploit his title for publicity purposes, he was obliged to work. Every evening, on returning from some reception to his third floor on the Square Laborde, the world's most famous gastronome sat down at his desk and took up his pen. He devoted all his energy to the furthering of culinary science. Collections of recipes alternated with gastronomical reports and prefaces for "*Livres d'or.*" At the beginning of the Occupation, Cur left Paris for Brittany where he found shelter with his old friend, Mélanie Ruat at Riec-sur-Belon.

Mélanie Ruat kept an inn that was one of the most renowned in France. Cur had helped and advised her when she opened it. He had discovered Mélanie one time when he was on a vacation. A widow with six children to support, she had set up one or two tables in her grocery-refreshment bar. On those humble little tables, Mélanie Ruat served food fit for the gods. The prince said so: he also wrote about it, with the result that, in two years, the grocery-refreshment bar became an inn that was classed among the high spots of gastronomy.

When, in 1939, Curnonsky arrived at Mélanie's, he asked for partial board.

"That's reasonable," said the good woman. "You eat only one meal a day."

"But especially," added Cur in embarrassment, "there is the danger that my resources may be greatly reduced."

"Prince...," Mélanie Ruat said simply, "when a man has helped to build a house, he certainly has a right to run up a score."

Curnonsky stayed at Mélanie's until the end of the war. The prince took advantage of his retreat to write his memoirs, the best and most picturesque imaginable[1].

Speaking of the future, Curnonsky wrote: "It is enough for me that my eminent position may have been useful to my feeble means, to the cause of Tourism and of gastronomy. And also that my compatriots wish to give my name some day to a little street in Angers between the castle and the cathedral. Yes, my name, definitely not my pseudonym, for in years to come the little Angevins might wonder what that old Pole was doing in their town—and they would not know the answer[2]."

---

(1) Published by Albin Michel.
(2) Curnonsky was buried in the Beauchamps cemetery near Taverny (Seine-et-Oise).

HE CLASSIFIED GASTRONOMES

No doubt, one day, Cur's best texts will be collected in an anthology. It would be only proper. According to him, gastronomy like politics has its parties and he classifies them as follows:

Extreme Right: devotees of the *grande cuisine*, that masterly, exquisite and complicated riddle which calls for a great chef and first class materials and which we may call diplomatic cookery; the cuisine of embassies, of state banquets, of palaces—though the cooking in palaces is frequently only a parody of it.

Right: supporters of the "traditional cuisine," those who allow only wood fires, food cooked long and slowly and who maintain that one dines well only at home with no more than six or eight, when one has an old cook who has been attached to the family for thirty years, a wine cellar "from before the Flood," brandies chosen by one's great-grandfather, a kitchen garden and a hen-roost of one's own.

Center: lovers of bourgeois cooking or of regional cooking; those who are quite willing to admit that, after all, one can dine properly in a restaurant and that there are still good inns and excellent hotels almost everywhere in France.

Left: partisans of simple "uncomplicated" cooking; the sort of "snack" you can "whip up in a jiffy" with whatever food you have on hand. Those people are satisfied with an omelette, a chop well seasoned, a sirloin steak cooked to perfection, a fricassée of rabbit, even a slice of ham or sausage. They do not rule out preserves and declare that a sardine in oil is quite attractive, and that string beans in cans are as good as fresh beans. They seek out the "little places" where the owner does the cooking himself. They praise country cooking and its amusing *vin du pays*. They are the nomads of gastronomy. For them especially the neologism "gastronomade" has been coined.

Extreme Left: Freakish, restless people, the innovators, those whom Napoléon would have called "visionaries," preferring exotic cooking and all foreign or colonial specialties. But what particularly characterizes them is that they like to invent new dishes. One also meets in those groups persons of great ability who are not at all disturbing; free spirits, with this difference, that the anarchists detest *bombes glacées*, a dessert too classic for their taste.

A Cooking course at the école d'alimentation

Eleven centuries have passed since that late afternoon when Charlemagne and his lords found shelter and food in an Ile-de-France monastery. Since then French cuisine has developed from century to century until today it stands first— the finest cuisine in the world, the most classic... and also the simplest.

Though the fifteen and twenty courses of state banquets, such as Talleyrand and Cambacérès gave, are a thing of the past, France still entertains her guests with royal splendor and a ceremonial pageantry that enchants kings, queens and heads of governments. When we catch the exquisite aromas of the traditional dishes in French cuisine, when the golden liquid of a Mersault or the ruby of a Gevrey-Chambertin sparkles in our wine glasses, I like to think we have not spent our time in vain.

GALA DINNER AT THE ÉLYSÉE PALACE IN HONOR OF PRESIDENT KENNEDY
(AT THE LEFT OF MADAME DE GAULLE);
AT THE LEFT OF GENERAL DE GAULLE, MRS KENNEDY

RECIPES

A

D

E

F

G

H

Q

R

S

T

V

W

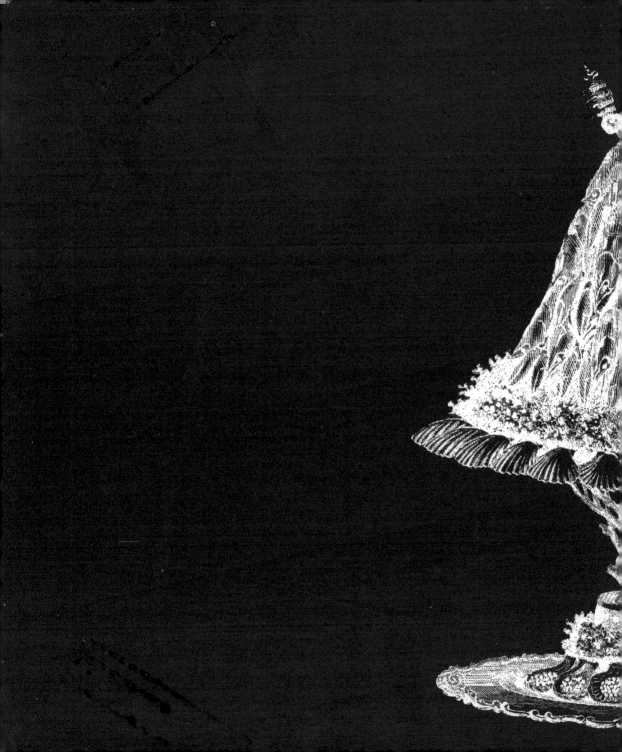